it dauned on me . . .

sprinkles of inspiration

it dauned on me . . .

sprinkles of inspiration

Daun Long Pittman

Rutledge, Alabama

it dauned on me…

Printed in the USA
ISBN - 9798699870691

This book recounts the events in the life of Daun Long Pittman according to the author's recollection and perspective. While all stories are true, some names and details have been excluded to protect the privacy of those involved.

Proof read by my dear friend Apreill Curtis-Hartsfield
Front and back Cover Photography – daughter PresLee Pittman
Devotion illustrations by daughter HeartLee Pittman

Thank you Tamekia Lee for inspiring me to finish my book.

Dedication

I dedicate this book of inspirations to the One who inspires me most, my Lord Jesus Christ!

And my two beautiful daughters, HeartLee and PresLee, my most amazing gifts from God.

Where do I begin to give the proper love and honor to my wonderful parents who have already gained their angel wings. Because of you, I have a personal relationship with God my Heavenly Father. Your Christlike example and love fill me with inspiration. Your prayers and faith help me to push through during the tough times. Your strength and giving hearts help me persevere and serve others. I wanted to keep you forever but…I am so very thankful that I had you for a little while. I will always cherish our special moments!

"I can do all things through Christ who strengthens me."
Philippians 4:13 – Mom's favorite verse

"A righteous man who walks in his integrity;
how blessed are his children after him."
Proverbs 20:7- Reminds me of my dad!

Forward

To be an encourager is to motivate, uplift and reassure, to boost and strengthen. What you fill yourself up with…will pour out. My desire as a Christian young woman is to inspire others to see their worth and to never give up. In my mom's book, she not only gives spiritual insight but speaks life in everyday situations. She has taught me to be thankful in good and bad times. Her Christian walk has allowed me to see what a Christlike woman really looks like. I have learned with God, possibilities are endless and happiness, joy, peace, patience, kindness goodness, faith, gentleness, self-control… are limitless.

My mom always calls me her Life Saver, but I call her my Hero. I am so thankful to have been raised in a family that taught me the importance of being a light and shining positivity in a sometimes – dark and sad world. There is no doubt in my mind that this book of inspirations will touch your heart and make it smile.

"I love you Momma, and am so proud to have you as my encourager."
Love, PresLee

Romans 15:13 "*May the God of hope fill you with all joy and peace as you trust in Him, so that you may overflow with hope by the power of the Holy Spirit.*"

I always begin my day with a cup of coffee in one hand a devotional book in the other that my mom has usually given me. Nothing brings as much joy, peace, and fulfillment as starting each day spending time with my Savior. I look forward to the daily scriptures and quotes that my mom sends to motivate me and encourage me to help and inspire others. My mom will forever be my rock and my stability. I have been taught the importance of trusting God and having faith no matter what trials and tribulations come my way. My mom has touched so many hearts and her book will continue to change many lives.

Thank you, Momma, for exemplifying every characteristic I hope to demonstrate to others around me and to my children one day. I love you and am so proud of your accomplishments!

Love, HeartLee

Introduction

In 2016, my family had been going through a rough season and I was searching for direction from God. I began focusing on Him more and I would say, "Speak Lord, I am listening." And… He did! He spoke in subtle ways throughout my day. Whether I was stomping in mud puddles in my rain boots, watching a carousal go around and around, or eating chocolate covered cherries, there always seemed to be a message hidden underneath. It's kinda like a God wink or a whisper but, I say a God sprinkle. No matter what you call it, I was filled with an overwhelming inspiration to write about it. So…I did!

You will read personal stories about my family, friends, and all my many pets. You will not only get to enjoy some happy moments but also experience some of the deep, dark, and broken places. None- the- less your heart will be inspired.

Many of the stories in my book were inspired by the special students I taught throughout the years. That same year I felt led to write Bible verses on the top of my hand every morning before class began. Initially, I wanted to look down at my hand throughout my day and be encouraged. Soon, all my students wanted to do the same. We used colorful, washable markers, and memorized lots of scripture that year. Everyone asked the students about the writing on their hand whether they were at school, in the grocery store, or a home. What started out as something so little…became a big testimony about God. Many of the stories in my book were inspired by the special students I taught that year. So, even the young at heart can relate. As the pages flow across your fingertips, allow God to touch your heart, renew you mind, and refresh your soul.

Deuteronomy 32:1-3 says,

"Listen, O heavens, and I will speak!
Hear, O earth, the words that I say!
Let my teaching fall on you like rain.
Let my speech settle like dew.
Let my words fall like rain on tender grass,
Like gentle showers on young plants.
I will proclaim the name of the LORD.
How glorious is our GOD!"
God's Word refreshes the soul.

it dawned on me...

That rainy days do not have to be dreary days. As a Kindergarten teacher, I remember singing the old song, "It's raining. It's pouring. The old man is snoring. Bumped his head, fell outta bed and couldn't get up in the morning."

I know the feeling! When I hear the rain beating down on the roof at 6:00am, I do not want to roll out of bed. Gray clouds are dreary, depressing, and lifeless in a rainy-day kind of way.

On a happier note, while rain is not the most popular type of weather, it is essential to the survival of every living organism from plants to animals to humans. Rain is quite refreshing and gives us an opportunity to be fashionable. Purchasing cute rain gear for my daughters each school year, inspired me to get some rain boots of my own. I did not realize how much easier rain boots made my life during messy weather. Having these protective boots on gave me the desire to intentionally jump into puddles because I knew my feet would not get wet. It made me feel like a kid again.

Oh, the freedom to just let go and enjoy the moment. Think of it this way, in all the rain and puddles of life, try to show your passion and jump in with both feet. Make a big splash, take a risk and get dirty. Do not hold back.

Fresh ideas pour down like rain leaving behind puddles of inspiration. Hosea 6:3 says, "*He will come to us like rain.*" Rainy days do not have to be upside down days. Remember, gray skies will eventually clear up and the sun will appear. So, turn your frown upside down and put on a happy face.

it dawned on me...

That trees represent powerful symbols of growth and resurrection. When I was a little girl, I remember visiting my grandmother and climbing her fig tree. This was in the olden days when we actually played outside.

It was a huge tree and we enjoyed eating the figs during our visits. Figs were my mom's favorite. Years later my dad planted a fig tree in our backyard, and it grew to an enormous size. My daughter HeartLee enjoyed climbing when she was little as well.

One summer night a storm came, and lightning struck the old tree splitting it right in half. We thought our fig days were over. For several years, the tree looked very sad and in the natural eye there seemed to be no hope. My dad just left the tree alone. It was still.

A few years later we saw a miracle take place. The fig tree began to produce figs again. It was like the dead tree had come back to life. How amazing it is that after years of brokenness, God restored the tree and it flourished. My dad always allowed his friends to bring a bucket and fill it up full of figs. That is just how he was!

Another interesting fact about a tree is the shedding of leaves. Trees were not designed to face cold weather or snow before releasing their leaves. In other words, trees were not made to carry more than they should. And neither are we! Refusing to release often means refusing to have peace. Like a tree we cannot carry the weight of two seasons.

Do not miss out on the joy each season promises to bring. As the wind whips by you today, hear it whisper… r-e-l-e-a-s-e. Not only can a tree teach restoration, a tree can show us how lovely it is to let the dead things go. So, "*Be still, let go, and let God!*" Psalm 46:10

it dawned on me...

Without the slider on my corkcicle, better known as my insulated tumbler, it just does not stay cold or taste fresh anymore. I mean, just that one, tiny, little piece fell off, flipped under the couch, and it affects the whole thing. I casually looked for the clear piece. No luck!

Just saying, in everyday life, could God be that missing piece we so desperately need and are searching for? That piece needed to enjoy and truly live a satisfying life? He wants to meet us at the intersection of every dream, every desire, every choice and every thought.

He is the calm in our chaos, the peace in our panic, our rock! And He is not hard to find. Psalm 23:2 says, "*He leadeth me beside the still waters.*"

There is nothing more refreshing than soaking up the sun and relaxing by water that is gently flowing. It is a place where you can breathe deeply and get a little R&R.

Psalm 23: 3 says, "*He restoreth my soul.*"

Yes, Jesus is that missing piece that we so desperately need, and He is as close as the mention of His name. "*The God of all grace, who called you to His eternal glory in Christ will Himself restore, establish, strengthen, and support you after you have suffered a little while.*" 1 Peter 5:10

Someday we will find what we are looking for or maybe we won't. Maybe we will find something much greater than that. Jeremiah 31:25 says, "*I will refresh the weary and satisfy the faint.*"

it dawned on me...

This is exactly why I use a Filter on my pics before posting. Meet Penelope, my dog. First picture is the result of her indulging in some chocolate covered coffee beans over the holidays. Second, a filtered and beauty setting photo of the beautimous Miss P.

I am only being silly. My Penny came from the animal shelter and although she is the most hyper dog I have ever met, she is super loving. She loves life and truly believes that everyone that comes to our house is there to visit her. I could not refuse her the first day we met at the shelter.

She came in like the Tasmanian Devil, knocking over several drinks and candles in the office. At first, I wanted to high- tail it and run! But just look at that face. What a difference filtering makes.

More importantly running the things we inhale through a God Filter helps ensure our exhale is our divine best. Philippians 4:8 serves as a spiritual filter for any and every area of our life. "*Whatever things are true, whatever things are noble, whatever things are just, whatever things are pure, whatever things are lovely, whatever things are of good report if there is any virtue and if there is anything praiseworthy meditate on these things.*"

I will filter my life with Your Word. I am beautiful because God says I am. Does it really matter what anyone else thinks? 2 Corinthians 3:18

it dawned on me...

That this red-hot, spicy candy that I bought my music students did not only light my mouth on fire it ignited a flame of red-hot inspiration!

This Tongue Torcher, so cleverly named by the way, was difficult to maintain. The longer you could endure the pain and not give up the easier and sweeter it became.

My students enjoyed playing different games near the end of class time. The winner of this game would be able to withstand the challenge of keeping this fiery piece of candy in their mouth the longest. Oh, what fun! Reminds me of the story in the Bible of Shadrach, Meshach, and Abednego. They were the Hebrew men thrown into a fiery furnace by Nebuchadnezzar, the king of Babylon. You see they refused to bow down to the king's image.

The three are preserved from harm and the king sees four men walking in the flames. The fourth was the son of God! Fire is consuming, burning, bright and hot. It is used to shape, refine, purify for heat, for light. We should pray that God will set a fire within us so that He can change us into the person that He wants us to be.

Yes, this transition may be painful for a short time. We need to push through and allow the Holy Spirit to move and have His way in our heart. Then we can experience an everlasting, sweet freedom. We will become a beacon of light, an inspiration for all to see.

I love what John 3:30 says, "*He must become greater; I must become less.*" Lord, please rekindle the fire of Your love in me.

it dawned on me...

That sometimes our words lose their flavor. In passing we say, "Good morning, how are you?", "Nice to see you.", "Haven't heard from you lately."

Big Daddy and Big Mother

We send random texts and sometimes type empty words, numb words, "just to be nice" words. Sadly, my words. Do not get me wrong, it is important to greet one another, especially with a big smile. It is not that these words are bad. It's just, sometimes they become habit and feel meaningless.

Colossians 4:6 says, "L*et your speech be always with grace seasoned with salt, that you may know how ye ought to answer every man.*" If we have Christ in our lives, then inspiring words should pour from our lips.

Years ago, I remember visiting my grandparents during the summer. They did not have air conditioning and it was always extremely hot. But there was nowhere else I would rather be. My only memories of my grandfather, Big Daddy, were of him sitting in a recliner by a fan that was in the window. He never said a word. My mom told me that he was a man of few words and if he ever said anything, it would be extremely important. Kinda like E F Hutton. Lol

When he finally did say something, you better believe, everyone listened. His words must have been seasoned with salt. They must have had great value and meaning. If only the words that we speak were of great worth.

Lord, may you seal my lips so tightly that my words can never slip out. Paralyze my hand so that my words are never written and sent. Make my words no longer exist and allow Your words to fill this vessel. God, let Your words soar through me like a light bursting forth in the darkness, without me ever even making a sound. Father let my words be lasting words, nourishing words, words of love, hope, joy, truth, and comfort. Words that feel, words that heal, words that change lives and make a difference. Your Words. Jesus may others walk away feeling better than they came because Christ lives inside of me. Psalm 12:6 says, "*The Words of the Lord are Flawless.*"

it dawned on me...

Adam Wallace

I am a perfectionist when it comes to things I really enjoy. It is easy for me to get super frustrated if things do not turn out exactly the way I expect them to. I want it to be perfect in my eyes.

This way of thinking can cause anxiety and frustration. It reminds me of one of my favorite Kindergarten students I taught years ago. We were learning to write letters and numbers. Every time he wrote a letter on his paper, he immediately would erase it. It looked perfect to me, but evidently it was not perfect in his eyes. He would write, erase, write, erase and so on and so on.

Adam was an extremely clever student but would not get finished with his work because it did not turn out exactly the way he wanted it to. I recall how shocked I was the day I was told that Adam had Leukemia and would possibly miss several months of school. I remember visiting him at the Children's Hospital and helping him with his homework when he was home. His mother, Debra and I were extremely close, and we were expecting nothing less than a miracle.

I am blessed to say that Adam is healed, and all grown up now. Funny story that happened that year in K-5. My sweet Jessica said, "Adam can run a million!" Then strong-willed Turner said, "No, he can't, only God can!" Lastly, quiet Jonathan said, "…and He-Man!" hahaha!

Many often feel discouraged because they have not reached their full potential. God is perfect, and He wants us to be like Him, right? But what happens if you were to achieve perfection. Do you stop there? It is imperfections that keep us alive, motivating us to push further and further. Each time you conquer something, there will always be another challenge waiting.

This is your journey and life is your mirror! What you see on your outside always comes from your inside. My kindergarteners enjoyed singing, "He's still working on me, to make me what I ought to be." In fact, Ephesians says it like this, "*For we are God's masterpiece.*"

So, don't be so hard on yourself. Relax, trust in God and let Him do the perfecting. (I find it quite interesting that, He-man's real name is Prince Adam.)

Sadly, my sweet Jonathan recently passed, and my condolences go out to his family and friends.

it dawned on me...

That I do not have 20/20 vision anymore. When I was in second grade, I was excited to receive a Mrs. Beasley doll for Christmas. I still have her today. She was the favorite doll of Buffy, on the American comedy series, *Family Affair.*

Mrs. Beasley was quite unique because she could talk, and she wore a pair of glasses. Oh, how I wanted a pair of glasses too. I would wear Mrs. Beasley's glasses and pretend they were mine. Thankfully, I now own my own pair of glasses and do not have to borrow hers. LOL

For me, one of the most annoying things about growing older is losing my ability to see like I used to. Now, if I am at the grocery store and forget my glasses I must ask, "Who just waved at me?" So, no offense, if I act like I don't know you; it's because, I don't!

This could be a good thing. My life verse is found in 2 Corinthians 4:8, "*Fix our eyes not on what is seen, but on which is unseen. Since what is seen is temporary, but what is unseen is eternal.*" This is a difficult verse to grasp hold of. It is important to focus on the eternal glory because it far outweighs any difficulty we are presently facing.

Focusing on the unseen is faith and faith pleases God. Truly there is no lasting satisfaction with things that can be seen. Amazing things like faith and the power of the Creator which cannot be seen, brings eternal gladness. 2 Corinthians 5:7 says, "*For we walk by faith, not by sight.*" This means we live by believing and not by seeing!

So, I would like to encourage you to get rid of your glasses today. Let the world become blurry and begin to clearly see…that God has not forgotten you!

it dawned on me...

After all these years, how happy I am to have kept my Winnie-the-Pooh. He was my very favorite stuffed animal of all time. I slept with it every night and drug it around with me everywhere as a kid. I sometimes neglected and forgot about him, but Pooh was always there. He was a little tattered and torn but did not look too bad for his age.

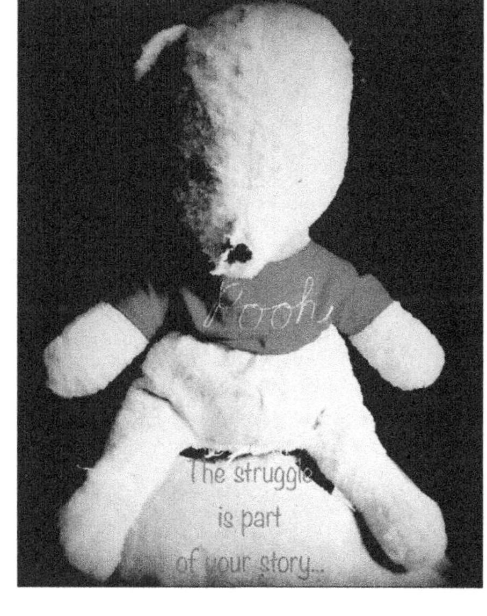

I actually restuffed him three years ago. I just got too busy to mend his nose and sew the ear back on. Some of the stuffing is hanging out and the poor thing has only one eye. But that does not change my love for Pooh.

Reminds me, after all these years, God kept me too! Sometimes I neglected and forgot about Him but, God was always there. He was never too busy to wipe my tears, heal my wounds and put my brokenness back together. Even at my worst when I was a mess, it did not change God's love for me.

You may be tired and worn with a heavy heart. Your soul may feel crushed by the weight of the World. Just know that God did not bring you this far to leave you. He will keep you and will restore you because He loves you.

Good advice Christopher Robin gave Pooh: "You are braver than you believe, stronger than you seem, and loved more than you'll ever know." Romans 8:38 says, "*For I am convinced that neither death nor life, neither angels nor demons, neither the present nor the future, nor any powers, neither height nor depth, nor anything else in all creation, will be able to separate us from the love of God that is in Christ Jesus our Lord.*" You are loved forever!

it dawned on me...

Every time I see a chandelier I want to jump up, grab on, and start swinging. I want to break out in song:
"123, 123, pray
123, 123, pray
123, 123, pray"

(of course, my words are a tad different than the original version)

Sure, I would love to swing from a chandelier, and act like tomorrow doesn't exist. I'd like to fly like a bird in the night, while God dries the tears from my eyes. Honestly, that is not a bad idea!

The Bible clearly teaches that tomorrow is promised to none of us, that each day is a gift from God. We wake up day after day and simply take for granted that we have tomorrow, when in reality, tomorrow is not guaranteed! I will never forget standing next to my younger brother's hospital bed in shock. He looked exactly like my dad did on the ventilator so many times before. Little did he know that after church he would collapse while playing soccer and his heart would stop beating. Thankfully, a nurse was at the game with her husband and began aggressive CPR. In fact, it was so aggressive that he ended up with four broken ribs and a broken sternum. But this is what saved him.

Wow! God put a nurse at the scene and firemen from across the street also came to his rescue. I envisioned seeing Jesus standing behind my brother with his hands on his shoulders as he laid in the hospital bed. I imagined angels gathered around him praying. It gave me great peace in knowing that David was in God's hands.

It is so important that we make the most of this day. This day can be as special as you want to make it. What if we made an effort to pray more, love more, give more, and cherish more? Let us not take even one day for granted because when it is over, it is never coming back.

You may be young and healthy this morning, but you easily could be a corpse by sundown. Sad, but true. How amazing it would be for us to dream like we will live a hundred more years, but to live each day like it is our last. In Luke 9:62 Jesus says, "*No procrastination. No backward looks. You cannot put God's kingdom off till tomorrow. So, Seize the day!*"

it dawned on me...

PresLee

Winning is everything! I mean, you work so hard, you give it your all, and you put your whole heart and soul into it. And then, you come up short and do not take home the first- place prize. I know, I know what you are thinking.

Doing your best is what is important. Sure! But when you lay it all on the line, it really does not feel like it. Getting past the initial pain of what feels like everlasting defeat is easier said than done. Sometimes losing hurts, but it does not have to harm us. The key is where we set our minds and hearts.

The ability to look beyond our disappointments determines how we face victories and defeats in life. I remember one year my daughter, PresLee made the girls basketball team. She was the tallest player but certainly not the most aggressive one. The coach did not have her as a starter, and she was a little nervous when he would put her in the game. The team had not won a game that season and the fans were growing a little weary from all the losses. I will never forget this one particular night. The score was tied, and the fans were cheering loudly. The other team would score and then our team would score. You could feel the excitement in the room.

I was a tad nervous because PresLee was on the court. The time on the clock was running out and we were two points behind. There were only a couple of seconds left in the game and the ball landed in my daughter's hands. She was nowhere near the goal, yet everyone shouted, "shoot it!" That was the day my heart stopped beating for a couple of seconds too.

Well, PresLee did just that and scored a 3 pointer which won the game! I remember jumping up and dropping my purse through the bleachers to the ground. The crowd was screaming, and the gym was on fire! The players lifted her in the air. What an amazing win! It felt like we had just won the national championship! And it felt so good.

Colossians 3:1,2 says… "*Set your mind on things above, not on things on the Earth.*" This way of thinking looks to Christ instead of earthly accomplishments that only feel good for a moment.

What is truly important is the One who measures how we have done in life. If we live for Christ, then we are winners! And we will win the ultimate prize on this side of heaven.

Yes! With God as our focus, winning is everything. And winning feels so good. Success is not final, and believe it or not, failure is not fatal. It is the courage to continue that counts.

it dawned on me...

That I may not know which way to go, but God does. And all I really need to do is simply just ask Him. Proverbs 3:6 says, "*Seek God's will in all you do, and He will show you what path to take.*"

Recently, I had to make some big decisions in my life and of course I went to God about it in prayer. But I was not exactly sure what God wanted me to do. I guess I just wanted to hear God speak out loud or see the answer written in the clouds. God can answer any way He wants to but most of the time we just need to step out in faith.

Not always so easy, especially when purchasing a new home, accepting a new job, getting hitched, making a big move, etc. Sometimes taking a leap of faith is scary. But I have learned if fear knocks at your door, then let faith answer it.

I remember desperately needing a job with good benefits and thankfully had several interviews. I was extremely excited to interview at a teaching job for students with autism. I thought this was right up my alley. After all, I taught for 30 years. I spent the day observing and loved every minute of it. It broke my heart when I found out that they chose someone else for the job. I just could not understand why God would allow this job to fall through.

But I learned very quickly that sometimes rejection is God's protection. After 15 months of praying for a job, God opened the door. You see, He had been working behind the scenes all along. He was preparing the way and putting the right people in the perfect position. Had I not

waited and trusted God, I would not have met my dear friend, Julie, who opened the door for my interview.

This new job not only provided great benefits and wonderful coworkers, it also allowed me enough freedom to focus on God throughout my day. When you develop a close, intimate relationship with the Lord, He will be your guiding light. He will open the doors that need to be opened and close the ones that need to be shut. The key is to move and trust God. He is a good God and wants what is best for you. If you stick with Him, He will guide your every step. His way is perfect.

May you find comfort in knowing that My living presence will accompany you on your journey. "I walk beside you, in front of you, and behind you. The wind that brushes across your shoulder is a gentle whisper…I will never leave you." God

it dawned on me...

That my favorite emoji is the heart. I use it continually when posting. Luv, luv, luv it, can't get enough of it! I had my first child when I was 34 years old and I wanted to pick the perfect name.

I had taught so many students over the years, so I wanted something unique, something different. During the summer months, I remember watching soap operas with my mom. There was a handsome young man on The Young and Restless named Hart, and I knew that was it. When I found out she was a girl I decided to spell it like this...Heart.

When my dad heard my plans, he was not extremely thrilled about it. He said that he never heard anyone naming a child after an organ in the body. So I decided to make it a bit more personal. I added my grandmother's middle name to it and named her HeartLee Dannell. Her middle name was a mixture of my dad and mom's names combined, Dan and Rosa Nell. Of course, my dad loved it!

You know, everything flows from the heart. Your hopes, your dreams, your fears, your anxieties, your anger, your forgiveness, your humility, your peace, your greed, your generosity, and your love also flow from the center of your being. Everything that makes you who you are is in your heart. And the crazy thing about your heart is that it is where the predator, the deceiver likes to reside.

So, do not be enticed for he comes only to steal, kill, and destroy. He is the father of lies. Resist and pray often. Proverbs 4:23 is so important. "*Guard your heart above all else, for it determines the course of your life.*" Our minds and heart are intricately connected so what we dwell on in our minds affects our inner spirit and heart. The Bible tells us to think about things that are pure, and right, and heavenly. Philippians 4:7, 8 says, "*Fix your thoughts on what is true and honorable, and right, and pure, and lovely, and admirable. Think about things that are excellent and worthy of praise. And the peace of God, which transcends all understanding, will guard your hearts and your minds in Christ Jesus.*" When HeartLee learned to write her name, she wrote it with a heart, then Lee. How sweet! She is a blue-eyed lefty just like her Grand Grand (my dad).

it dawned on me...

That I am a kid at heart! I am truly drawn to the beauty of the carousel. The lights and sounds are magical. How exciting it is to choose an exotic animal to ride upon and to spin and spin like you're seven years old again. Every time my daughters and I shop at the mall, we find it difficult to pass by the beautiful carousel without buying a ticket and taking a fun ride.

After all the spinning and drunkenness of the magical ride, here is a sobering thought - What goes around, comes around. This means that the consequences of one's actions will have to be dealt with eventually, for those of us who wrestle with sin. Sometimes sin comes in beautiful packages and enticing intrigue. And just because Jesus paid for it does not mean that it is excused in our life. It still has consequence and we need to bring it readily to God. Sin is never hidden from the eyes of God.

Sometimes the hardness of our heart thinks that our sin is not a big deal and that it does not have a cascading effect on those around us. But our sin almost never happens in a vacuum. Our sin almost always affects us, and it affects our relationship with God. Sin will more often than not, contaminate those around us.

Everything you do, everything you say, every choice you make, sooner or later comes back around.

Hebrews 12:1,2 says, "*Therefore, since we are surrounded by such a great cloud of witnesses, let us throw off everything that hinders and the sin that so easily entangles. And let us run with perseverance the race marked out for us, fixing our eyes on Jesus, the pioneer and perfecter of faith.*" The wonderful news is that we may fail God a thousand times, but His mercy always remains. And when we stumble again and again, we are caught in His sweet amazing grace.

it dawned on me...

That the more you hang around, communicate or get to know someone, the more you begin to act and think like them. You both may say the same thing at the same time, or they may text you when you were just thinking about them. You may even end up wearing the same color clothing on the same day.

When you spend a great deal of time with someone you may even pick up certain habits, sayings, and expressions. I remember my best friend Debbie's unique laugh back in high school. It was amazingly different. It was kind of like a high-pitched scream that lasted several seconds. After a few months of spending time together we were both laughing like little screaming pigs in her bedroom over boys and teenage things.

I also remember a time when I got in the habit of saying "oh, my God." My mom's sweet friend, Mrs. Vivian Wall, told me that she once had the same problem, so she began substituting the word "lands" for "God" and it helped her break the bad habit. So, I began saying, "oh, my lands!" I can still hear Wanda, one of my closest friends in college, saying the same thing.

There is just something special about those we hang out with and we rub off on each other in good ways and sometimes not so good ways. As Christians we are to strive to have the mindset of Jesus. And what a beautiful mind it is.

If we have the love of Christ in our hearts, developing a Christlike mind is not a daunting feat. It is something we should desire and strive for. Romans 12:2 says, "*We are transformed by the renewing of our minds.*" One method we can use to renew our minds is to meditate on God's word.

Dig deep into the pages of God's Living Words, memorize scripture, and pray, pray, pray. Find the time and energy to connect with God on a regular basis, just like you would with any relationship that mattered. Soon you will begin to act more like Him and speak His Words. You will be focusing more on Him and picking up Godly habits. Others will see a difference in your expressions.

Who knows, maybe you will even dress like Him - lol. When Christ's mind dominates our mind, then we will truly be in our right mind.

it dawned on me...

That I am just a teeny, tiny speck on a tiny dot in this miraculous universe. Yet, God knows me. He knows my name. He knows the number of hairs on my head. He knows when I sit down and when I rise up. I am known.

In fact, Jeremiah 1:5 says, "*Before I was formed in the womb God knew me.*" Psalm 139 says, "*For You created my inmost being. You knit me together. I was sculpted from nothing to something.*" Guess what? You are known too.

It is so interesting that there are more stars in our universe than there are grains of sand on all the deserts and beaches on earth. I heard it said like this, the earth is just a tiny dot on God's finger, and we are a teeny, tiny speck on that dot. That is how big our God is. There is nothing too big for Him to handle.

I'm a tiny dot on a tiny speck in the universe

There are about 1 billion trillion stars in the observable universe! Yet, God calls them all by name and He knows them all by sight. It says in Psalms that the sun, moon, and stars praise Him. Can you imagine what it is like way up there in the sky? It must be like a sea of light proclaiming His Majesty.

It is amazing how One so great could care for you and me. We serve such an amazing God. One who placed every star in the sky and called them all by name! How much more is His love for us? Long before you were conceived by your parents, you were conceived in the mind of God. Job 10:12 says, "*You gave me life and showed me Your unfailing love.*"

We may be small in comparison to the God of the universe, but all life has dignity and value in His sight. There is no greater honor than the privilege to love, live, and praise God for the rest of our lives.

it dawned on me...

I luv, luv, luv all the glitz and glamour of rhinestones, sparkling bedazzlement, sprinkles of glitter on everything. The more the better, the prettier, whatever! It is fun to put rhinestones on fingernails and cheeks, glitter on the eyes or spray in the hair. Bling is always a hit!

When I was a majorette in college, we never entered the football field without sparkling from head to toe. Years later, my dance team did the same. We always sparkled and shone!

When I was a little girl, I remember thinking that my grandmother, whom I called Mama Long was a queen. She was almost six feet tall and wore at least 3-inch heels. When she stood up, she held her shoulders back and walked like she was on the red carpet. Dr. Chandler, a previous family pastor and chiropractor said that she had the best posture and straightest back of anyone he had ever met at her age. At the time she was in her 80's. Every time he walked past me at church, he would pat my back and remind me to sit up straight. Needless to say, when I saw him coming, I sat up as straight as a board every time.

Mama Long, Bobby, Big Mother

My grandmother always had on a dress with a matching purse,

necklace, and earrings. She was always sparkling. It was so much fun visiting because she would always share her make up and jewelry with me. Such fond memories.

But is bling the real thing? This reminds me that there is a lot of counterfeit out there. Even in their beauty, rhinestones sometimes fall off, break or get lost, and glitter gets messy. Tears sometimes flow down to streak our cheeks and nails may chip. It's all gotta go when the clock strikes midnight. POOF! It disappears!

Many times, we do seek the bling bling stuff. I remember many years after my grandfather passed, my shorter grandmother, about five feet, married a millionaire, so to speak. He gave her a 5-carat diamond ring. It was huge! Several years after his passing, she gave it to me, and I put it in my jewelry box.

During one of my desperate moments, I sold some of my gold and most of my jewelry to the jewelry store. Sadly, I found out that the 5-carat diamond that I was depending on for help, was only a cubic zirconia. Seriously? The store manager said that I would be amazed at how many men buy cubic zirconia instead of the real thing.

Anyway, it taught me a great lesson though. I should not depend on anything but God. My grandmother is now married to Bobby. He likes to be called Uncle Bobby. He is such a great man of God and has such a gentle spirit. God in His infinite wisdom knows what we need most… His authentic love.

So, do not be blinded by the shiny, fake, bling that the world has to offer. It is here today and gone tomorrow. Those little fake gemstones who cowardly love only for a moment and walk away. Plastic pearls who use, abuse, manipulate, and shatter the heart yet continue to smile. The glass diamond, the silent killer, who cuts, robs the soul and leaves only feelings of inadequacy.

It is important that we seek the real thing…God's love! Nothing can tarnish it. And at the stroke of midnight, in your despair, your prince Jesus will come and find you. Hebrews 18:8 says, "*Jesus Christ the same yesterday, and today, and forever.*" This means that yesterday He loved you, today He loves you and Nothing will ever change.

it dawned on me...

Since I am horrible with directions, I always follow others when traveling to both my daughters' extracurricular activities. This was before I had an i-Phone with Mapquest, of course.

I was on my way to a game and knew that I had better pay attention to my surroundings because I would be coming back alone! Being the not-so-observant person that I am, I managed to follow another parent's vehicle, which by the way was going way over my speed limit. They left me like dust in the wind.

I knew I had better look for signs along the way. I made a right turn past a school and then proceeded to drive out into the boondocks. It was getting a tad dark, but I was able to vaguely see an old torn down looking store. It had a bent Pepsi sign dangling from a pole, and I made a left turn. Still venturing out into the middle of nowhere, I continued my journey, praying that I would make it safely to the game.

Earthly signs are temporary and can be misinterpreted, misread, or not seen at all. But a relationship with God is permanent and He wants to lead us on our journey. We must look to God for wisdom through prayer and scripture. He can give signs in mysterious ways or simply through His word and through people. No matter what crossroad or dead end we face the Holy Spirit will guide us, and we can rest in the knowledge that we have not made the decision of which way to go in our own strength and reasoning.

On my way back from the game, I found comfort in seeing that old wobbly Pepsi sign because I knew that I was on the right track. But there is even greater comfort in knowing that God is always with us, leading, guiding, and directing which way we should go.

Sometimes we want big directional signs from God, but He just wants us to pay attention. Psalm 32:8 says, "*I will instruct you and teach you in the way you should go; I will counsel you with my loving eye on you.*"

it dawned on me...

In my weakness He is strong. 2 Corinthians 12:9 says, "*My grace is sufficient for you, for my power is made perfect in weakness.*"

Once I had the rug pulled out from under me, in such a way that I thought my life was over. I did not want to kill myself, but I did want to die. The pain was unbearable, and nothing would stop it. All I could do was lay at the feet of Jesus.

My emotions were a bit unstable though. One moment I would be standing tall, filled with faith, and then crumble to the ground in the same breath. My emotions were like a rollercoaster.

God sent someone my way just in the nick of time who taught me a simple prayer to help me through some of the most difficult moments of my life. When my feelings and emotions were just too hard to bear, I was told to lift my hands way up high towards heaven and say, "Lord, please take this emotion from my soul. Lord, please heal my soul. Lord, thank you for my healing." I prayed this prayer over and over and it helped tremendously.

Funny story - one day I was driving my car, and my heart was flooded with sadness and anxiety over a family situation. I lifted my hands in the air and said. "Lord, please take this emotion from my soul. Lord, please heal my soul. Lord, thank you for my healing." I immediately heard a beeping sound from the dashboard of my car. The words, "please put your hands on the steering wheel" popped up.

Jesus is only a prayer away

You may feel like God cannot see or hear you right now. You may feel like all hope is gone, and that you are hanging on by a thread. Your faith may be broken into a million little pieces and possibly you have been stripped of everything you know. You may cry out, "I am too old God, my life is over! How could you allow this to happen to me?"

Sometimes you see failure, but God sees victory. God sees in you what you cannot see in yourself. We see problems, He sees possibilities. Genesis 16:13 says, '*You are a God who sees me.*" So next time you are overwhelmed with life situations, let Jesus take the wheel. He is only a prayer away.

it dawned on me...

That the sun in all its radiant beauty, and glorious, flaming brilliance, reminds me of a glowing medallion in the sky. In fact, I was blinded by this celestial fireball today, while driving home from the State Drama competition. Some of my students received a shiny medallion for their glowing performances.

Speaking of things that glow, I remember helping decorate for school dances when I was a teacher. Hanging the disco ball in the center of the gym was always a big hit. On one occasion, the mirrored ball was not secured enough, and it plummeted to the ground. It was damaged but thanks to my handy, dandy, hot-glue gun, I was able to fix it good as new. The kids were so excited to experience beams of light flashing over them and seeing myriad spots of light dancing around the walls of the room.

The disco ball is roughly a spherical object that reflects light directed at it. So, in other words, it will not illuminate unless a spotlight is directed towards it. When light reflects on these mirrors, it is scattered in many directions, producing a novel effect.

The same thing happens when the light of Christ reflects on the mirror of our heart. We illuminate Christ and shine love to others.

I remember cleaning house one late afternoon. I was at one of my lowest moments and had just asked God where He was. I opened my daughter, HeartLee's bedroom door, put her clean sheets on her bed, and turned out the light. Suddenly, I saw hundreds of tiny, shining stars on her ceiling. It looked like a starry night outside. With tears in my eyes, I laid on her bed, mesmerized by the beauty of it all. I knew God had answered my prayer. He was right there with me all along.

God never intended for us to be blinded by the light, but to be overwhelmed with His love from the inside out so the radiance of Christ would shine bright from our lives. Daniel 12:3 says, "*Those who are wise will shine like the brightness of the heaven, and those who lead many to righteousness, like the stars forever and ever.*" Trying to shine on your own can be very difficult. He just wants us to be closely connected to Him and remain in Him. When we do, His light pours forth through us in power, brilliant ways that change the world!

it dawned on me...

That when we hurt…God hurts. Psalm 56:8 is such an amazing verse to me. It says, "*You keep track of all my sorrows. You have collected all my tears in Your bottle. You have recorded each one in Your book.*"

It is interesting to know that there are tear catchers made from blown glass that do just that- catch tears. Tear bottles were common in Roman times when mourners filled small glass bottles with tears and placed them in burial tombs as symbols of respect. During the Victorian period those mourning the loss of their loved ones would collect their tears in bottles with special stoppers that allowed the tears to evaporate. This symbolized the mourning had ended. In some American civil war stories, women were said to have cried into tear bottles and saved them until their husbands returned. The tears showed the men how much they were loved and missed.

Mom and Dad

This reminds me way back when my dad was in the Vietnam War. My mother, older brother, and I lived with my grandparents, Big Mother and Big Daddy. I was too young for school but my older brother, Danny, who was 9 at the time, was excited to go to the same school that my parents once graduated from. I will never forget sitting out on the front porch and shelling peas and butterbeans. I remember one night at the dinner table my grandmother offered me some of those veggies. I politely said "no thank you, I'll take a can of chicken noodle soup, please."

It was very peaceful out in the country and we would sleep with the windows open at night. I slept with my mom and fell asleep to the sound of crickets chirping. My dad had given my brother some military equipment like, canteens, helmets, masks, etc. and he and my cousin Eric always pretended they were warriors in combat. I wanted to play too so they always let me be the nurse.

I noticed that my mom watched the news constantly that year. I remember saying, "Mom, why do you watch the news so much, to see if Big Danel dies?" I think she was shocked that a little four-year-old would ask such questions. I've noticed lately that my sister-n-law Sharon calls my brother Danny, Danel too.

Every time I see Big Mother, my 99-year-old grandmother, she tells me the story about my dad sending me tape recordings and telling me not to give her any sugar/kisses. He wanted me to save them all for him on his return. She never fails to mention how I stuck my dirty foot up in the air and told her she would just have to kiss my foot instead.

Those were the days my friend. My mom cried many tears that year while dad was gone. I am sure God was catching every one of them. It encourages me to know that God cares that much about me and you to collect our tears in His bottle. Just know, that whatever you are going through, God does see you and mourns right along with you.

1 Peter 5:7 says, "*Let your tears fall onto His hands; He cares so much about you.*" I remember vividly, every night my mom would take my brother and I into the bathroom, light a candle, and say a prayer for my dad. Thankfully after 365 days of candle burning, Dad was home safely.

it dawned on me...

I am the representation of Heaven. God's message has never been the problem. The problem has always been the messenger. As Christians, we have exclusive rights to the greatest story ever told, which is the gospel of the risen Savior! It is very important to live a Christlike life because we may be the only Bible some may read.

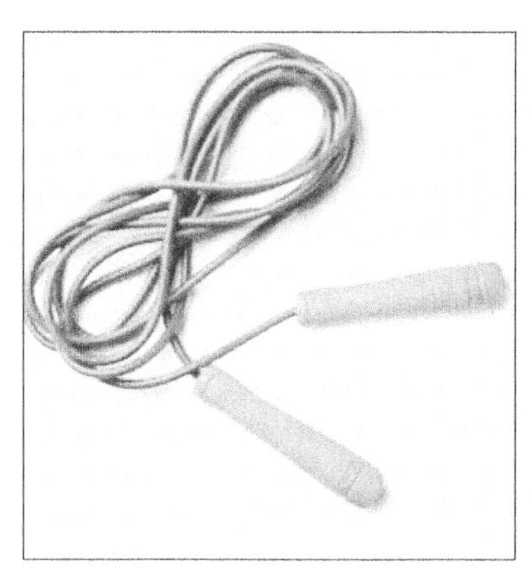

We should strive to be the hands and feet of Christ. Help my words to be part of the answer, not a part of the problem. May everything I say somehow glorify God. I have a duty to lay down my opinions and what I think and say what God wants.

As far back as I can remember, I found myself taking up for people in my neighborhood or at school. When I was in first grade a bully was going to hit my friend with a jump rope and I remember grabbing that rope and telling them in a stern voice, "If you hit her, then I am going to hit you." I ended up getting into a little trouble taking matters into my own hands though.

One time in high school some students were making fun of a girl before class began and everyone was laughing. I was so angry at them and sad for her. Too bad I did not have that jump rope, I would have been turning tables over and whipping everyone out the door, like Jesus did to the money changers.

It wasn't easy, but I got up out of my seat and went over to her and bent down and told her not to listen to them because they were stupid and did not know what they were talking about. I tried to make her feel better the best way I knew how. Years later I saw her somewhere and she needed a ride. She remembered that day and thanked me.

Wow! God is amazing! I have always been for the underdog and my daughters are no different. I think that is what compassion looks like. Jesus was filled with compassion and He fought for those who had no voice. He also had empathy. Empathy is giving grace to someone when you do not have to give grace to them – where it is not deserved. When you feel like judging remember You are an ambassador of Christ. It does not mean that you hold back on truth, but the way you say it changes forever.

it dawned on me...

As I sat there and watched some leave the game before it was over, I began to realize that they were giving up a bit too soon. I mean it did look as if there was no hope for a win, but with God all things are possible, right?

Sometimes we face things in life that seem too difficult and we throw our hands up as if to say, "I give up!" What does giving up actually look like anyway? I think giving up is accepting things the way it is instead of fighting for it.

I can remember fighting one of my most difficult battles through prayer. I did not just pray casual prayers, I prayed critical prayers. I prayed about my circumstance daily for a couple of years. If it is of any importance you will continually pray until it comes to pass. The sad part is that some become weary and began to feel like there is no hope. They lose that desire to push in and sometimes sadly give up. They throw in the towel, so to speak.

Remember, when you can't.... He can! It is important to give it to God. Lay your concerns at His feet and let Him fight your battle for you. Exodus 14:14 says, "*The Lord will fight for you; you need only to be still.*" It is not that you are giving up, but you are giving it to God and trusting Him with the outcome.

So, when faced with a challenge hang in there. Do not leave the game early. Even when the scoreboard says it is over, it is not over yet! Remember it is by God's power and He is working. He is supernaturally, orchestrating things that our minds cannot comprehend.

So, sit back, relax and trust that He is in control. God sees the bigger picture and His ways are much higher than ours. His winning is sometimes different from our winning. We may win the game by losing, at least from the scoreboard's standpoint.

Isn't that what happened to Christ? He lost His life, but it was a part of the coach's plan. God was working everything out for the good, rearranging things, behind the scenes, on the court of life. So, when the clock is running out and the buzzer finally sounds, those who follow Christ will bring home the win! It is not over in this game of life. Our God is the God of instant second chances!

it dawned on me...

That not being picked can be heartbreaking. Have you ever anxiously waited for the moment to come when the list of names was to be posted? Your heart was overwhelmed with excitement and breathing was not even an option. You barely had the courage to look and when you peeked, your name was not there.

Or, what about the time you worked so hard to make the team, but were not chosen? There may have even been a time when your friends picked favorites and you were overlooked. I was a military brat and my dad was transferred to a big city where I attended a huge school. I was very excited to try out for cheerleader and worked diligently for months to prepare. I had always been a cheerleader and could not wait for tryouts to finally get here. There were so many girls trying out and I was shocked when I found out only 2 sophomores could make the squad. I remember practicing in my backyard.

I would run and practice my round off, split, and jumps in the grass. I meant that I was going to make this team. Boy, I sure was heartbroken when the results were announced, and my name was not called out. It felt like the world had ended. I felt like a failure. There were many broken hearts in the gym that day. I remember going to the movies a couple of days later and one of the senior captains saw me and told me that I made alternate and that if someone dropped the squad, I would be pulled up to take their place. My heart sank. I was so close!

But it was good enough news to make me feel so much better. That is how God works sometimes. He puts people in the right place at the right time. And that is what He did for me. Rejection is a hard pill to swallow. But remember this, it is okay if your name is not on the list and you did not get the part, or you were not chosen on the team, and not picked by your friends.

You may have been overlooked by everyone else, but you are handpicked by God. You are chosen by God meaning, you are His first pick and His best choice. Yes! You will suffer disappointments in this life, sometimes repeatedly. But you need to remember that as a child of the King, this rejection is a momentary bump in the road. Your rejection is God's protection. You can either allow the bump to derail you or you can choose to claim the heritage of the child of God and move forward in grace. The only true thing you can do is to try over and over again. When you fall get back up. When you get rejected, don't get stuck, try again.

God has not overlooked you. He has something amazing in store for you. Remember His timing!

it dawned on me...

That if I had a hammer today at the grocery store, I would have given that big stuffed animal claw machine a whack! Do you know what I am talking about? The kind you put your loose change in and maneuver a big claw-like thing over all the animals. You try and grab the cute one on top that does not look as if it is lodged between any others. The tricky part is getting a tight grip and lifting it in the air without it falling.

Well anyway, two little girls in line before me ran over to the machine. The first girl dropped her money in and grabbed that animal as quick as lightning. She held her prize high in the air and ran back to her mom giggling so happily.

With a look of excitement, the second little girl dropped her coins in. With the joystick she drove the claw down on to a cuddly pink bear with a t-shirt on and gently picked it up. I was so amazed that I was about to witness two wins on a machine that usually gulps up all your money. As she moved the claw to the left to drop her win in the slot, the bear slipped through the claw clutch and landed back into the pile with all the other animals who were waiting to be adopted.

The little girl immediately ran back to her dad. I could sense her pain and he gave her a little pat on the back and proceeded to ask the cashier for a dollar back in change. I noticed that he tried several times to win that pink bear for his little girl.

This reminds me of our Father's love for His children. He really wants to give us the desires of our heart. He watches over us and is quick to help us in every situation. If we ever fall, He is right there to pick us up and reassure that everything is okay. He paid our ransom that we could never pay. And now, He stands with open arms, inviting us into eternal and abundant life.

I do not think the little girl took home the prize that afternoon, but she skipped out of the grocery store holding her dad's hand smiling contently. At that moment she knew everything was going to be okay. Just like our earthly dad, our heavenly Father wants so much to give us the desires of our hearts. In fact, Matthew 7:11 says, "*So if you sinful people know how to give good gifts to you children, how much more will your heavenly Father give good things to those who ask Him!*"

it dawned on me...

Who is He with power that none can tame?
And who is He that every foe would fear His name?
Who is He who bore our guilt and shame?
Who suffered that dark day?
His name is Jesus and He is the lion and the lamb!

I read a story once about a little lamb who was crippled and had a limp. He had a difficult time keeping up with all the other sheep when they traveled to new grass land with their Shepherd. This one particular night, the stars seemed extra bright and the sheep were excited to go and eat some fresh new grass.

The Shepherd told the little lamb that he would not be able to go on this trip, for it would be far too long for him to travel. The little lamb was very disappointed and sad. He stayed in the barn as he was told.

Never in a million years did the little lamb know that he would get to witness the greatest birth on earth. The birth of Jesus Christ. The lamb thought he would be missing out by staying behind, when in reality God blessed him with the greatest gift of all, Jesus!

I love the fact that the Bible presents Jesus as both the lion and the lamb. What a perfect picture! How amazing that this lion, with all His power, came to earth as a submissive lamb. He was then led as a lamb to the slaughter and still bears on His resurrected body the effects of the crucifixion. Jesus is the lamb that was slain and the lion that reigns.

I read that sometimes our greatest fear in the world is the opinion of others. But the truth is, Gods opinion is the only one that really matters. And the moment you are unafraid of the crowd, you are no longer a sheep, you become a lion. A great roar arises in your heart, the roar of freedom.

I love this because it reminds me that I am God's lamb and He gently cares for me and loves me. When I'm lost He finds me and tenderly carries me. God's opinion is the only one that counts.

It is important to keep my eyes on Christ and not on people or problems surrounding me, and just follow Him. Like a lamb He will not only keep me humble, meek, and compassionate but, like a lion, He will give me confidence and strength to boldly stand up to the crowd, and roar to the top of my lungs that JESUS IS LORD! No matter what anyone thinks. This is freedom!

it dawned on me...

That little things mean the most. It amazes me how eager others are to throw away their birthday cake toppers. Many take them and just plop them into the trash like they never existed.

Many moons ago, I thought my ballerina cake toppers were the most beautiful things I had ever seen. I had seven ballerinas and put on my own dance recital with them. I admired the beauty of their costumes, imagining that I was one of them dancing on center stage. In my eyes their smallness was greatness! I played with them often and still have a few of them today after all these years.

Sometimes we feel so small and unimportant here on earth. It is nice to know that we are valuable to God and it is this very fact that gives our life meaning. It is truly a miracle that the God of the universe surrounds our tiny, little lives with His loving care. Psalm 139 says, "*He knows my every thought even before I speak it.*" He knows exactly what we need to make us smile.

You may feel your life is grayish brown, small and unremarkable. But God wants you to know that you matter, and He sees you. He loves you with His everlasting love and He alone knows all about you and every hope and dream you hold so dear. He knows the issues in your life and how it will turn out. In fact, God sees the big picture. He knows the beginning to the end. Just yield to Him and trust Him. You may feel small but in God's eyes you are great! Like my ballerinas, God cherishes you and gazes at you with graciousness and favor. You are His beloved.

it dawned on me...

That my daughter, HeartLee takes after her momma. She loves to dance and make up routines like me. She took many years of dance lessons and she is quite the choreographer.

I can remember staying super busy when I was a little girl too. I took dance lessons on Monday, baton lessons on Tuesday, was a Brownie on Wednesday, and a cheerleader on Thursday. Needless to say, I was a jack of all trades. I was born a teacher. I would teach all the kids in my neighborhood dances and even gave free baton lessons. I did not have enough batons to go around so I unscrewed the sticks from our crochet set and had enough sticks for all to participate. We even had recitals in my back yard.

My friend Bobby concocted a curtain hanging from a tree that could be opened and closed, and that was our center stage. Everyone dressed in all my dance costumes. We handed out tickets and even had refreshments, BBQ Fritos and water in Dixie cups. Those were the days!

When HeartLee was five, she would wear all my dance costumes and perform for everyone who visited. She even ventured out and performed at friends' homes. Funny, whenever we visited my best friend Anji, her husband would go to another room to get away from all of us women. We could always find HeartLee dancing and performing for him as he rocked in his rocking chair. She was born a performer...still is!

As I have gotten older, I have gotten a bit clumsier at times. Once I slid off my seat during music class and missed the stool when I sat down

at a production. I have even tripped over the music stand during class and missed my chair on the way down. What else can one do, but just laugh along with everyone else.

I have learned though, if you stumble, it's ok, just make it part of the dance. Ecclesiastes 3:1-4 says, "*To everything there is a season, and a time to every purpose under the heaven. A time to weep, and a time to laugh; a time to mourn and a time…to dance.*"

it dawned on me...

Skylar Mask

I want a childlike heart. Matthew 18:3 says, "*Truly I tell you unless you change and become like little children, you will never enter the kingdom of heaven.*" A child is simple and uncomplicated. They are like sponges that soak up everything God says and truly believe every word of it. There is something so wonderful about how trusting and openhearted a child is. They see others through the eyes of Gods unconditional love.

I remember something miraculous that happened during my second year of teaching Kindergarten. During Bible time I was teaching my students about Jesus healing the ten men with leprosy. Jesus was traveling along the border between Samaria and Galilee. As He was going into a village, ten men who had leprosy met Him. They stood at a distance and called out in a loud voice, "Jesus, Master, have pity on us!" When He saw them, he said, "Go, show yourselves to the priests." And as they went, they were healed. One of them, when he saw that he was healed, came back, praising God in a loud voice. He threw himself at Jesus' feet and thanked Him.

My students loved this Bible story. We always closed our Bible session with prayer requests and prayer. This was a very special time indeed.

One day during recess, several students noticed a hurt bird lying on the playground. Frantically, they ran over to me and said "we must pray for the bird to be healed." They grabbed my arm and took me to what looked like a huge, dead buzzard. It was not breathing and literally, I was petrified!

I told my students that this poor bird had already gone to birdy heaven. This made them more persistent to see it rise up from the grave. There was nothing I could do or say, so I prayed. We all held hands and gathered around the bird and I began to pray.

In my mind I said, "God, please help me. These kids are expecting you to do something." I believed that Jesus could, just did not know if He would. To be quite honest, I did not have the faith needed for this poor bird to rise again. Oh, but my students did! After I desperately prayed that God would heal the bird, we began to softly chant, "I believe Jesus can, I believe Jesus can!" Suddenly, the bird moved. We all gasped for a moment and then began to shout, "I believe Jesus can, I believe Jesus can!" In our amazement the bird jumped to his feet!

By this time, we were pounding our fists in our hands and screaming, "I believe Jesus can, I believe Jesus can!" We were amid a full-blown miracle. We were all so amazed to see the bird fly up on top of the school's roof. We were jumping up and down, crying and hugging each other, when my student, Langdon said, "Wait!" He continued by saying, "Now we need to thank God for healing the bird, just like the man with leprosy did after his healing." So, that is exactly what happened.

While we prayed a prayer of thanksgiving, the bird flew away into the sky. Look what our God can do! Oh boy, childlike faith is extremely powerful. You see children never doubt, they only expect miracles to happen. It is because of their faith that God moved! A child not only has great faith, but such a forgiving spirit. A child's heart is so tender and eager to forgive and love past the stains of hurt.

Being like a child in this way is a perfect picture of what it means to be a strong, responsible, mature, Christian adult. It means having so much faith in our Daddy that we can rest and be content. Being childlike is like love and sunshine, so good for the soul! Childlike faith along with childlike love are an open road to God's heart.

it dawned on me...

Kristin Long

Running is not easy. I tried so hard to become a runner like my sister-in-law and her family. I was in awe of the medallions they had won, the numerous races they participated in at Disney World, and the fashionable running outfits too. Running was the hot topic at all the family gatherings, and I wanted so much to be able to participate in those conversations and be able to call my runner friends peeps on social media.

So, I began training and found that the hardest thing about running for me was the breathing part. I had to literally focus on correctly breathing the whole time. I could not jam out listening to music or talk with a friend on the phone, or even run my dogs. No, no way! Breath control was the only thing on my mind. Breathe in my nose, out my mouth, in my nose, out my mouth. I wanted to give up because it was so difficult, but I persevered. My breathing did get better with time and I ran my first 5K. Even though I did not win, I was excited to get a T shirt and post pics for all my peeps.

No matter what challenge you face, never give up, even if you do not bring home the crown. Lean into God and push through, no matter what your goal is, continue to fight. When you chase after God's purpose for your life, you may run in to delays. God uses those waiting periods to prepare and test us so that we can face whatever is coming in the next phase of our faith.

When everything else is unknown, God is our known. He is the one we can rely on and hold on to. What God has in store for us is better than anything anyone else has to offer. If you feel like giving up or that you cannot make it, do not forget what Galatians 6:9 says, "*So let us not get tired of doing what is good. At just the right time we will reap a harvest of blessing if we don't give up.*"

"*Everyone who competes goes into training. They do it to get a crown that will not last. But we do it to get a crown that lasts forever!*" 1 Corinthians 9:25 So, you did not win the crown? But did you really lose? Life is about impacting others, the choices we make, and the way we choose to view the situation. God is more interested in what you are becoming… than what you accomplish. "*Be faithful…I will give you the crown of life!*" Revelations 2:10

it dawned on me...

My Family

That although putting puzzles together can sometimes be tricky, the pieces, when placed in the perfect position, can create a beautiful picture. Putting puzzles together on family game night was something we loved to do.

There would be two puzzles scattered out on the table and each family member would take turns seeing who could put the puzzle together first. Sometimes it was disastrous if a piece were missing or someone threw a tantrum for losing. Oh well, family fun, right?

Many years later, I remember a time when my broken pieces were not only shattered but scattered and destroyed. I was in a place of silent desperation. Unable to lift myself from the ground, I tried to grab hold of a few broken pieces to somehow salvage, I guess. This is it. This is what rock bottom looks and feels like. I did not want to kill myself, but I did want to die. In the natural my situation was hopeless. It would take a much greater force than I had in me to attempt this colossal puzzle.

Matthew 19:26 says, "*Humanly speaking, it is impossible. But with God, all things are possible!*" No matter if you feel like your heart is broken into a million pieces, you are not alone. You may feel hopeless and abandoned. Maybe you feel as if your life is completely over. You may have lost every ounce of strength you once had and find it difficult to breathe.

Just know this, God can gather all the pieces of your brokenness and put it back together again. He will rebuild your life for the better and make you complete in Him. Malachi 4:2 says, "*For those who fear His name, the son of righteousness will rise with healing in its wings!*" Whatever we endure, His care is certain. His love is unfailing, and His promises are secure.

Broken things can be blessed things if we let God do the mending. Jesus can transform our hearts. He knows how to put every piece back together and positions them in the perfect place. God sees the beautiful in us even when we are in a million pieces.

it dawned on me...

That kids imitate what we do. My hair is long, and I tend to pull it over to one side. I am not exactly sure why, it must be a habit, I guess. The sweetest thing happened today during my 2nd grade music class. When we started singing and dancing, I noticed one of my girls with her hair swept to one side just like mine. She made sure to keep it there.

Lydia Sowell

I said, "I love your hair that way." She said, "thank you but It's hard to keep it here." Got to love her!

Reminds me of the importance of being careful what you do and say cause there are seeing eyes all around. And those seeing eyes may imitate you. Ephesians 5:1 says, "*Imitate God, therefore, in everything you do, because you are His dear children.*"

The people we spend the most time with are the ones we become most like. It has been said that true character is revealed by what someone does even when no one is watching. So, it is time we start imitating our Father continuously and demonstrate His love to those around us. Remember, you may be the only Bible someone ever reads. Someone may go where you go. Someone may say what you say. Someone may hear what you hear. Someone may do what you do. Make sure your imitation will be worth the risk!

it dawned on me...

That my name should be Dr. Doolittle. These guys follow me everywhere. They are my hairy children, my pets.

No matter where I go or what I do they know everything about me. They know when I sit, when I stand, and when I eat. They trust me and depend on me and need my constant attention.

All day long they put their hope in me to take care of them. So, I pat them on their heads as if to say, "I am here, no need to worry." At times they get on my last nerve but…I love them anyway.

How comforting it is to know that wherever I go, God is with me. Joshua 1:9 says, "*The Lord my God will be with me wherever I go.*" Even if I cannot sense His presence, He is paying attention to me. He walks with me and talks with me. He knows when I sit and when I stand. Every moment He knows where I am. He places His hand of blessing on my head. For He is the God who saves me. He is my only hope! At times I am so undeserving of His love and compassion but… He loves me anyway.

it dawned on me...

A smile does not tell the entire story. Sometimes we cannot capture the pain and fears that are hidden behind those beautiful curved up lips. Everyone has a story, so it is important that we take the time to look, really look, at those around us. Their books may not be completely open for us to read. But we may notice that their pages may be worn, and the edges may be a bit frayed.

Philippians 2:3-4 says, "*Be humble, thinking of others as better than yourselves. Don't look out only for your own interests, but take an interest in others, too.*" We need to be compassionate and patient because ultimately, we do not know what obstacles they have overcome and what they may be going through. Some may seem to have it all together with a beautiful smile, hair and make-up intact and nice attire.

Others may be unlovely, unlovable, and annoying. But as Christians, can we truly look past the outward appearance with a Godly sensitivity and possibly see a scarred and broken heart on the inside? John 13:34 says, "*As I have loved you, love one another.*" How hard can it be to consider others before ourselves? The Bible also tells us that the second greatest commandment is, "*Thou shalt love thy neighbor as thy self.*" Mark 12:31. And He is not just talking about our actual next-door neighbor. He is referring to anyone we meet daily.

If we could make loving others a priority, imagine the difference we cold make in the lives of so many. There are many ways to show love and concern. A warm hug, a loving smile, a gentle pat, a kind word, a helping hand, a fervent prayer, a simple call, a verse of hope, a thoughtful gift, a loving visit. Loving God empowers us to love others. The focus on love helps us not settle for a minimum concern for our neighbors, but to truly reach out to them.

Spreading love to others helps take our focus off our own concerns and problems. The heartbeat of God's love gives us the power and motivation to serve Him. This love will explode from our hearts and we can, in turn, love others. Romans 12:10 days, "*Be devoted to one another in love, honor one another above yourselves.*"

Yes, we have all struggled at times and we've probably all judged a book by its cover. But judging a person does not define who they are, it defines who you are. We may be the only Bible anyone reads so it is important to shine Christ's love throughout our pages. May we be His hands and feet here on earth so that others can catch a glimpse of Jesus. Let God be the author of your book and it will be a best seller!

it dawned on me...

That it is not too difficult to brighten someone else's day. One of my best friends' mother is one of those people who goes out of her way to help others.

Years ago, when spending the night at my friend Anji's house I noticed all the many kind things her mom did not only for human beings but creatures as well. She would bake cakes and treats, make T-shirts and pillows and share with others. She cooked meals for my parents and other families when they were going through strenuous situations. Her vehicle took the place of a taxi service, picking up people for church, and women's conferences.

She was always there for people, especially those less fortunate. I saw her pick up baby possums, whose mother had been killed, from the road and feed them with baby bottles. She did the same for squirrels too. Her son, Tom took after his mom when it comes to squirrels. I will never forget the day when one of her squirrels started chasing Anji and me. We took off down the hallway and the squirrel flew on my back. Needless to say, I am super petrified of those little guys now.

Anji is a lot like her mom, very talented, giving, and compassionate. I do not know what I would do without her friendship. Proverbs 27:9 says, "*A sweet friendship refreshes the soul.*" She is definitely the sister I never had. Wouldn't the world be a better place if each of us would sprinkle a little kindness on someone every day. I once heard that ARK stands for "Act of Random Kindness". So, I thought it would be neat to attempt a personal act of random kindness each day. It could be just

Joyce Dix, Anji and Daun

a smile, a kind word, or a simple homemade gift. Whatever! It is the thought that counts, right?

Kindness makes you the most beautiful person in the world no matter what you look like. When I think of kindness, I think of a warm fuzzy feeling. When we are kind, others get to experience that warmth too. And whether they realize it or not they are experiencing some of God's character. Jesus Christ is the greatest, most complete picture of kindness we will ever know. God saw a lot of hurt, brokenness, and despair so He sent His Son to the rescue.

There is really nothing more attractive than someone who goes out of their way to make life beautiful for someone else. Our days are happier when we give others a bit of our heart rather than a piece of our mind. I would like to encourage you to sprinkle a little joy on others and leave a glitter trail of kindness behind you everywhere you go. Believe in the magic of kindness and Sprinkle, Sprinkle, Sprinkle!

it dawned on me...

That my earthly dad was a tremendous man of God! But why wouldn't he be? My grandfather Daddy Long was a powerful man of God too.

I remember visiting Daddy Long's home when I was a little girl and listening to him pray in the spirit at night while I was in the bed. I was not afraid at all because I knew he was a Christian and served God. In fact, I do not believe I ever saw him in anything other than a suit. He was definitely a prayer warrior and someone to be admired. His son followed in his footsteps.

Though he never wore a tie, my dad was hardworking, giving, loved his grandchildren, and his sister, my Aunt Shirley. I don't think my dad ever missed a day of talking to his sweet sister on the phone. He and my precious mother planned to travel and visit military friends after his retirement. Sadly, a few months after, he had a massive heart attack which changed the direction of his life completely. We did not know if my dad would make it. His heart was damaged tremendously. He died several times on the table and was somehow brought back to life. It just was not his time to go yet.

PresLee and Gran Gran

Although it took many months for him to heal and get back to a somewhat normal life, doctors said he probably would not live past four or five years due to the extensive damage of his heart. My dad was so different now. He just sat around the house with no expression or determination. Before all of this happened, he was on the go constantly. I had my second daughter a few weeks before his heart attack and now that he was home recuperating, he never looked her way.

But as healing began to take place in his heart, I began to see healing in his hands. One day he jumped up from the sofa and picked up my precious baby and held her for the first time. I finally saw him smile. He held her all the time and never wanted to put her down. He held her close for the next 18 years!

Wow! What a miracle! Praise God! Proverbs 20:17 reminds me of my dad. It says, "*A righteous man who walks in his integrity; how blessed are his children after him.*" So, how is your heart today? Is it in need of some tender loving care, some mending, some molding and reshaping? If so, give it to the One who is the ultimate Physician, Healer, Rebuilder.

The condition of our heart is crucial. The heart regulates the hand. When your heart is right, you put your hands to the right things. Boy, am I blessed to have had the most amazing earthly father! Many years later my dad's close friend and Pastor, Dr. Malone Chandler, whom we love dearly, told me something quite interesting. He said that my dad asked God for 15 more years of life just like Hezekiah did in the Bible. God not only answered his prayer but gave him a few extra years. That is just how loving our God is!

it dawned on me...

That people will know me by my love. You see, love is an action. Love is something taken from me and given to you or taken from you and given to me.

I will never forget waiting to see my mother at the Rehabilitation Center on my birthday many years ago. She had been diagnosed with Transverse Myelitis at the age of 55. She lost all movement from the ribcage down. This was a life altering disease that required aggressive prednisone treatment. My eyes caught a glimpse of her big eyes and beautiful smile as she rolled in her wheelchair towards me.

She had something in her lap that seemed to ignite excitement in the room. She handed me the most beautiful handmade angel. It was made from paper and looked like a beautiful doll. It was my birthday present.

She was stuck in rehab and wanted so much to give me a gift. She always remembered special occasions. Someone in the Rehabilitation Center was making the angels and my mom was super excited to purchase one. She had the most giving and loving heart ever.

Although she was in rehab learning to walk again, regain strength, and just hoping to live a normal life… she only thought of others. On this day, she only thought of me. She was selfless. Selfless means that you are more concerned with the needs and wishes of others than with one's own. The greatest love is selflessness. It forsakes everything to giving up one's own life for someone else. After all, what could be a greater gift for someone to die in place of another?

Jesus laid down His life for us, to not only save us from our sins, but to demonstrated to us what real love is! My paper Angel remains on my dresser as a beautiful reminder of my Mother, who is now my Heavenly Angel. Psalm 23:6 says, "*Your beauty and love chase after me every day of my life.*"

My mother's favorite verse was found in Philippians 4:13, "*I can do all things through Christ who strengthens me.*" Though my mother suffered many years physically, she kept a smile on her face. Her strength made a great impact in the lives of others. I admire my mom's walk with God, and her ability to embrace life during good days and not so good days. She is my hero, my biggest earthly inspiration.

it dawned on me...

That my heart is God's home. When I was a little girl, I remember reading a story about salvation. In my mind I can still see the picture of Jesus standing at a door and knocking on it. He looked very patient but seemed quite persistent. Revelations 3:20 says, "*Behold I stand at the door and knock: if any man hear my voice and open the door. I will come into him, and will sup with him, and he with me.*"

I never really understood this verse until I was in the sixth grade. We began attending a church in Niceville, Florida. It had a wonderful youth program. I remember hanging out with my friends at church on weekends. We had food, fellowship, Bible study, and skating in the gym. That year my oldest brother, Danny, was the first in my family to get saved followed by my mom and dad.

God must have been knocking at my heart's door too, but it felt more like a tugging at my heart. Not only do I remember the overwhelming anticipation of wanting to go to the altar, which I now know was the Holy Spirit, I also remember the struggle to remain seated.

You see, I was extremely shy and to take that first step would have been out of my comfort zone. The struggle was real, but one Sunday night, I took a deep breath, went to the altar and asked Jesus to come into my life. He came into the darkness of my heart and turned on the light. He made Himself at home lighting a fire in the cold hearth. He started music where there had been stillness and filled emptiness with His own loving, wonderful fellowship. I have never regretted opening the door to Christ and I never will. Many years later after growing up

My Family

and having a family of my own, there were days I felt as if Jesus had left me. My once warm heart did not feel so welcoming anymore. After all, it is difficult to have a soft heart in a cruel world, right?

The fact is life is hard! You may be facing the tragic loss of a loved one, abandonment by a spouse, a child gone astray, loss of your home, or received a shocking doctors report. No matter what, during difficult times it is easy to invite bitterness, regret, depression, unforgiveness, to spend the night in our hearts home. A callused heart may protect us from great pain, but it also keeps us free from great love.

Proverbs 4:23 says, "*Watch over your heart with all diligence, for from it flow the springs of life.*" Yes, there will be difficult days but that does not mean God has abandoned you. He stays when everyone else goes! Take your pain to God and He will care for your broken heart. He will clean up the mess in every room, and mend your heart in a healthy way, free from calluses. Ezekiel 36:26 says, "*And I will give you a new heart, and a new spirit I will put within you. And I will remove the heart of stone from your flesh and give you a heart of flesh.*" Do not fail to allow God in because you are embarrassed at what He may see in your heart's home.

It really does not have anything to do with the condition of your heart. God does not want your ability; He wants your availability. If you truly yield your heart to Him, Jesus will inspire you and take control of your life. He will pick up what has been scattered about, and even rearrange things for your good.

God will give you a blazing transformation and uniquely enable you in ways you have never dreamed. My prayer for you today is found in Ephesians 3:17-20, some of my favorite verses, "*And I pray that Christ will be more and more at home in your hearts, living within you as you trust in Him. May your roots go down deep into the soil of God's marvelous love, and may you be able to feel and understand, as all God's children should, how long, how wide, how deep, and how high His love really is; and to experience this love for yourselves, though it is so great that you will never see the end of it or fully know or understand it. And so, at last you will be filled up with God Himself.*"

Rather than bandaging your own wounds, take it to God. He will heal and soften your heart and help you to love like He does. No one will ever love and care for your heart like Jesus will. In fact, Jesus is standing at your heart's door right now. Knocking, knocking, knocking, knocking. Will you let Him in today?

it dawned on me...

Dale Kline

The words "I love you" can be so healing. I cannot think of any number of words in the entire English language more powerful than these three simple words when said one after the other. They are calming, refreshing, and restorative. They speak healing, they are heartwarming, and they are encouraging.

Yet, some find it difficult to utter these words. Maybe because these words were not spoken to us as a child or we think that those words are not enough to express how we really feel. Some may think saying it over and over out of habit is meaningless. But having the habit of saying "I love you" would be a good habit to have. I do not remember my dad ever telling me that he loved me, but I do know that he did. He showed me by his actions. It was undeniable.

I wanted so much to hug my dad and tell him how much I loved and appreciated him, but was afraid to reach out and do it. I am very thankful that God gave me 3 extra months of quality time with my dad before he passed. After 18 years his heart stopped beating, but God brought him back for a bit longer. Thankfully both my mom and my dad were blessed with a wonderful caregiver, Dale, who took such wonderful care of them while they were at their weakest. My dad was back in rehab trying to recuperate and regain strength from his second major heart failure.

I was able to put him in a Nursing Home Rehabilitation Center near my home. Since I was teaching very early morning hours online, I was able to spend every day with him. I had prayed many months for God to remove fear of death and anxiety from his heart and mind. And God did just that. He had no worries or concerns while in the rehabilitation center. There was such a sweet spirit around him. I enjoyed our time together very much.

I had been searching for a house and planning on bringing him home with me to live as soon as he was better. During our time together I was able to hug him and tell him how much I loved him. It felt so good and was extremely emotional. While you still have breath in your lungs, I want to encourage you to simply say.... I love you.

It will make all the difference in the world not only for the other person but for yourself. I certainly wasted many years of holding back what I wanted so much to say. But I am extremely grateful God gave me extra time to fulfil my greatest desire, to love on my dad before he went to be with the Lord. Colossians 3:14 says, "*Wear love everywhere you go.*" I heard it is the popular new color this season!

it dawned on me...

I am not young anymore. Oh, the days of being so youthful, naive, and energetic. Trusting everyone and believing in everything. Making promises. You may remember crossing your heart and hoping to die. Please do not stick a needle in your eye. Not a care in the world. Happy – Go – Lucky! Soaking up life like a sponge and loving every minute of it.

Back in the day, when I was little, the big thing to do at a slumber party would be to prick your finger with a pin and become blood sisters. OUCH! It was so hard to do but oh, so worth it.

You see, I never had a biological sister and wanted one badly. But thanks to the good ole days I inherited several, wonderful blood sisters! What is it that is most appealing about children? Is it their openness to loving and being loved, or their playfulness?

Heartlee and Preslee

I believe that children possess something that many have lost – the quality of innocence. There is such beauty in childhood innocence. If we could just... Let it go! Let it go! Let all our worries go! Completely connect with God remembering that He completely loves us.

He knows everything about you and me and...loves us anyway!

He will give you the strength to face every problem you must deal with. And He will give you joy while you are dealing with it. Psalm 16:11 says, "*You fill me with joy in Your presence.*"

it dawned on me...

That my dog, Penelope, does not like rain or stormy weather. When she begins shaking from head to toe, nonstop, I know that bad weather is on its way. Her brother Hank never utters a sound until the first sound of thunder. Miserable are the stormy nights when trying to sleep with these two paranoid animals. One barking his lungs out and the other, shaking on top of my neck. True story!

But I thought about it and I honestly believe that my dogs are going through a dog trial, so to speak. This is their storm of life and they rely on their owners to protect them and keep them safe. Who knows what the poor things had to endure before being adopted by a family?

Storms come to test our foundation and will beat us to death if we are not grounded and rooted in Christ. Personally, I could live without storms, but the storms of life are inevitable. The winds will blow, the lightning will strike, and thunder will shake.

But you know what? I shall not be moved! You will not be moved! We will not be shaken! Psalm 16:8 says, "*I have set the Lord always before me; because He is at my right hand, I shall not be shaken.*" The only thing that should shake or move us is God's Word! Anything that is not grounded, great will be the fall of it! When the storms of life hit sometimes, we lose our balance and fall to the ground just like some trees do. Unlike trees, we must jump back up and keep going.

The world does not stop and wait for us to wallow in self-pity until we decide to move. Keep your eyes on God and let Him comfort and protect you. Stop barking negativity and fear. Trust the One who can calm the storm. Ephesians 3:17 says, "*That Christ may dwell in your hearts by faith, that ye, being rooted and grounded in love.*"

it dawned on me...

Valentine's Day can be difficult for many individuals. Some may not get a hug from their Valentine or receive a chocolate treat. Sadly, some people may feel alone because the one they gave their heart to is now gone.

Just remember, flowers fade, balloons fly away, and chocolate is really overrated. In fact, chocolate is here for a moment, then gone, but found again somewhere on your thighs.

Always remember that God's love for us will never disappear! And He does not just show love and give gifts on special occasions. Every day His arms are opened wide. His love never fails to notice His children. He is so in love with you and wants to be your Valentine. He is always readily available to you.

But even more than that He wants your heart. Your heart is safe and sound in His hands today. Jeremiah 29:13 says, "*You will seek me and find me when you seek me with all your heart.*" So, spend time reflecting on how much God loves you today. "*Though the mountains be shaken, and the hills be removed, yet my unfailing love will not be shaken, nor my covenant of peace be removed says the Lord who has compassion on you.*" Isaiah 54:10

it dawned on me...

Yes, I would like one please, one whole box of chocolates!!! Oh, how I love chocolate covered cherries. But I find it quite difficult to only eat one, or two, or three. I just love to bite a little hole in the chocolate and drink the liquid first and then chew and swallow the rest. It really does seem impossible to only have one.

Thankfully, my daughters buy me these delicious treats only once a year. And boy do I enjoy eating them. This reminds me of a story that my grandmother, whom I call Big Mother, would always tell us kids while visiting during the summer. My grandmother is now 99 years old so, her stories are from way back when. Her real name is Mamie Lee and she had three sisters and two brothers.

Back in the olden days many children were considered wealthy if they received a gift such as a doll or a truck for Christmas. In my grandmother's family's case, getting candy on Christmas morning was a luxury. My great grandparents would hide all the candy under their mattress and then pass it out to all the kids on Christmas morning. One day her oldest sister Daisy found the Christmas candy and ate a little bit every day until it was all gone. She secretly ate the candy as she worked right beside my grandmother in the field.

So, needless to say, on Christmas morning, there was nothing left for the rest of the children. Oh well… ho, ho, ho! Daisy felt bad about what she had done but told her brothers and sisters that the candy was soooo good.

I totally get it! Sometimes candy can be simply irresistible and impossible to resist!

You may be facing some real trials and struggles in your life and see no possible way to deal with those issues. But, Jesus said, "*With men, this is impossible, but with God all things are possible.*" Matthew 19:26 I have decided to cut the word "impossible" out of my dictionary because it is not in God's vocabulary. Yesterday's impossibilities are today's miracles!

I am encouraged by the fact that God specializes in the impossible. Faith in myself does not exist! I have learned that faith does not make things easy, it makes them possible. Luke 1:37 says, "*There is no problem, there is no hardship, there is no difficulty, that is too tough for God!*" Even Mary Poppins agrees. She even said that everything is possible, even the impossible.

it dawned on me...

The enemy's greatest joy is for you and me to feel worthless and empty, lonely and sad, depressed and forgotten. I want you to close your eyes for a minute and imagine anything valuable here on earth. Well, guess what? It is incomparable to how God feels about you.

Now think about diamonds. They are rare, beautiful, and highly prized. But they are nothing compared to how God values you! God calls His children 'jewels' Malachi 3:17, and jewels need to be skillfully cut by a master craftsman if all their latent beauty is to be revealed.

Let's say for instance, you have two stones that are alike in color and equally pure, yet there is a marked contrast between them. Anyone who deals with precious stones knows that the difference is due to the cut. One stone may have received 80 cuts from the jeweler's chisel, and the other only 8.

The stone that has suffered much is radiant, but the one that has had little effort expended on it is dim and lusterless. You may be going through an extremely difficult situation in your life; just know that your light affliction, which is only temporary, is working for you an eternal glory.

If only we could accept our trials with joy because they are not worthy to be compared with the reward, we will eventually receive when we stand before the Lord.

The hammer blows of pain and suffering are designed by the Master Craftsman to shape us into objects of spiritual beauty and worth. Because of His divine chiseling, we will soon begin to shine with His reflected glory. The results will be manifested not only now but throughout the eternal glory. Daniel 12:3

God has formed many diamonds, but He only made one you. You are unique! He made you because He wants someone exactly like you. He has plans for you. Ephesians 2:19-22 says, "*Whenever you feel unloved, unimportant or insecure, remember to whom you belong.*"

You may be feeling worthless right now. Life has thrown more at you then you think you can handle. Just remember, "*You are precious in my eyes and I love you!*" says God. Isaiah 43:4 You are so precious to God that He sent His son! Think of it like this. You are worth…a SON to die for!

it dawned on me...

Life is like a boxing match. And this is how it goes, "Introducing first, from the white corner, carrying the weight of the world, He hails from the Heavenly Realm, the One and Only, the Omnipotent, Omnipresent, Omniscience, Eternal. Holy, Champion of the world… God!"

"From the red corner, weighing heavily on minds, He hails from the darkness below, the adversary who walks about like a roaring lion, seeking whom he may devour, the utterly evil…Devil."

I will never forget my oldest brother, Danny, making me play games with him when I was a little girl. I actually knew how to play Chess at 5 years of age and was pretty good at it. We raced cars on a racetrack, played Hockey, and electric football. But one of my favorites was the KO Parker Brothers boxing game. There were two boxers in a rink and two controls. We boxed each other until one of the boxers fell backwards. This meant there was a knockout.

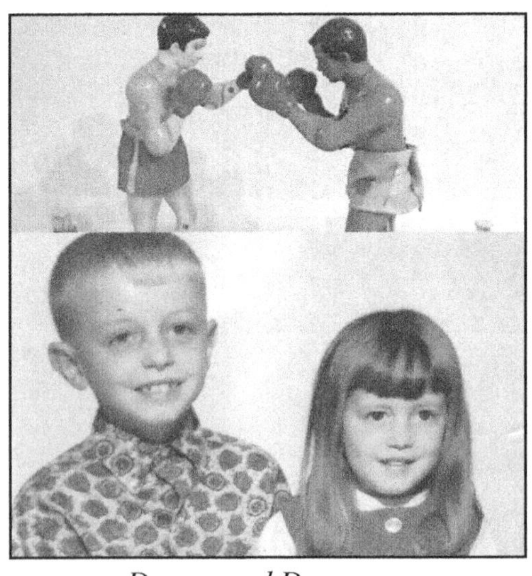

Danny and Daun

I can still hear my brother imitating the announcer. "In this corner…" lol This reminds me that not only is God on our side, He is in our corner cheering us on! Jeremiah 29:11 says, "*God is planning great things for our lives.*"

But Satan will quickly stir up storms before you as soon as you set out to sea. You try swimming upstream, constantly fighting a powerful current that seems to be pushing you downstream despite all your efforts.

But guess what? God controls the sails and has your enemy in His hand. You need not be afraid while you are being tossed about in rough, deep waters. No matter who or what is coming against you today realize, it does not have to make you sink.

God is your lifesaver. The storms in your life will only make you stronger and you will rise! Just do not lose faith and doubt in the very one who is for you and not against you. Your Heavenly Father will never disappoint you. He is the biggest, strongest, most loving person in all the universe, and He will never fail you. If you get knocked down, get back up. You will not drown. Jesus will breathe for you when the waves of life are overwhelming. When Satan attacks, do not ask, "Why God?". Just shout out loud, "Let's get ready toooo ruuummmble!" When the waves of life become more than you think you can handle, keep fighting and Float like a butterfly!

it dawned on me...

God can use us even in our heartache. I can remember during the most broken time of my life, my brother saying to me, "Go and serve someone who is in need. Get your mind off yourself and focus on God and what you can do for others."

At the time I could not fathom how I could possibly help anyone else in the shape that I was in. I could only think about myself. I was so selfish when I was at my lowest. My heart was broken into a million little pieces and I was self-absorbed. My heart felt like it had third degree burn. It was difficult to let past hurts go and my life seemed so out of control.

I desperately wanted to let my guard down and trust God somehow. After all, He can see the big picture, right? I knew God enough to know that He had my best interest at hand and that He could, but I was not sure if He would.

I learned a lot about faith during this time of my life. God taught me that faith was not believing that God could, faith was believing that God would. Oh wow! What an amazing lesson! Once I was able to pick myself up off the ground, I began to pray and ask God to send people my way that I could serve and minister to. This helped take the focus off my pain and uplift someone else who really needed it. I would look for others to serve.

I read about something called, ARK – which is an Act of Random Kindness, and decided to make this a part of my life. I asked God to send people my way to serve each day. As I began to serve others, healing began to take place in my own life.

1 Peter 5:10 says, "*And the God of all grace, who called you after you have suffered a little while, will Himself restore you, will make you strong, firm, and steadfast.*" So, take heart, the pain you experience today maybe your platform for ministry tomorrow. Of course, we all want to be restored and healed. No one likes to hurt or endure pain. But I think it is important to remain soft and pliable so that we can hear God speak. I pray this simple prayer every day so that I can be sensitive to the Holy Spirit.

Prayer - Lord, give me enough hurts to keep me human and enough failures to keep my hand clenched tightly to Yours. You tenderly minister to the shattered places in my heart. I am so grateful you can use every heartbreak in my life for good. I am choosing to believe today that You are leading me to a place of strength and victory. Amen

it dawned on me...

Michelle, Daun, Sharon

That I am known, and you are known too. We are important, even when we do not feel important.

Several months ago, before our world stopped turning due to covid-19, I was honored to be asked to be a breakout leader at our Women's conference at church. I found it interesting that our breakout group assignments were special words like *joyful*, *loved*, *chosen*, *redeemed*, *hopeful*, *faithful*, *gracious, blessed, called*, and my group was *known*. I think it is extremely important for us to realized that we are all known by God. Jeremiah 1:5 says, "*I am known*".

I remember when the pandemic first hit, and many were in a state of panic. I really was not phased so much, not because I did not take it seriously or think it was not real. It's just that I had already been going through a pandemic so to speak in my own life. Many of you had too. Maybe you have been abandoned or betrayed, received a bad doctors report, or lost a loved one. You may feel empty, forsaken, and hopeless.

But there is someone who sees you and will help you through the difficult times. There is purpose in your pain. You may feel unknown.

But it is extremely important for you to realize that you are known by God. In fact, Jeremiah also says, "*I knew you before I formed you in your mother's womb. Before you were born, I set you apart.*" So, what is this verse saying?

God loves you and has a wonderful plan for your life. It is not too late, and you are not a mistake! He knew you before you were ever even thought of. Trust in God and keep your eyes on Him. And remember, you do what you can, and God will do what you can't!

God was not surprised at all about this pandemic. He knew it was coming because God is all knowing. He sees the whole picture from beginning to end. And your circumstance comes as no surprise to Him either.

So, when circumstances are out of your control, lay it at the feet of Jesus. When you feel no one notices, know that someone does notice and that someone is Jesus. He loves you. He longs to be gracious to you. He rises to show compassion to you. You are enveloped in His comforting grace. You are never lost in a crowd because you have captivated Jesus' heart. His gaze is always fixed on you. He sees your pain and is aware of your affliction. Your circumstance comes as no surprise to Him.

Come as you are with all that makes you feel less than. Draw near to Him. Soak into His presence. Wait expectantly for Him and hear Him speak. I do not want you to forget for one second that you are known, and that God loves you. He has a purpose for your life no matter who you are, what you have done, where you have been, or how old you are. You are known!

it dawned on me...

What redemption feels like. There was a time when I felt nothing. I was completely numb and lifeless. Living in this dark world was empty. Watching the days and nights pass me by. Having conversations with myself. Literally believing "this is life". "This is what life feels like." "Life meant nothing."

But then, there was this connection, an intersection, a collision, so to speak. It left a crack in the tattered walls and a hint of light began to peek through. This ray of hope shined on the broken pieces and miraculously this heart…felt. It was a fresh, breath of new life. It was as if someone breathed new air into these lungs. This new awakening felt warm and safe.

Forgiveness and compassion flowed generously through my veins. Longing to spend time in the Word. Suddenly, I felt something. Excitement and joy began to flow, and I felt such expectation. Life meant something! That something makes me smile.

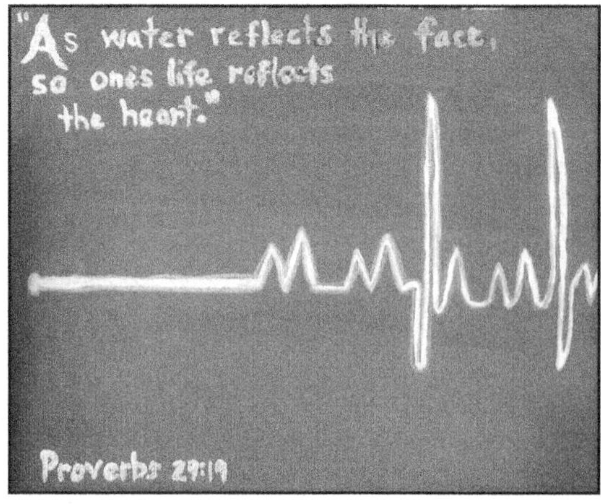

I remember the desperate cry of my sister-n-law, Kristin, when I received her call. I could hear the ambulance siren in the background as she said, "Daun, you need to get up here…it's bad!" I was so shaken; I couldn't figure out what to wear, but thankfully my daughter came to my rescue. All I knew was that I had to get to my brother. I knew God had this, but I felt myself unraveling. I also could not figure out how to pray either, but thankfully the Holy Spirit came to my rescue.

My brother David was hooked up to every machine imaginable. He was in the fight of his life! His heart stopped beating, there was no pulse, he was lifeless.

But God was not finished with him yet. He put all the right people in the right places at the right time! He breathed new breath into his lungs and fresh, oxygenated, blood flowed to his heart. When I left the hospital the first night, I had a vision of Jesus standing at the head of the hospital bed with both hands on my brother's shoulders. There were also Heavenly angels hovering all around him. This gave me tremendous peace.

The next few days were critical, and hundreds, possibly thousands of people were praying for this man who had been an inspiration to many. I told God if I could only have one miracle then please let it be my brother's healing. My prayer was a little selfish because I really didn't know how to live without him. My daughters and I especially needed him at this particular time in our lives, but I knew his family needed him more.

God gave us a miracle and I felt reassured I would have the opportunity to be the encourager and strength provider for him as he had been for me and my girls for so long.

it dawned on me...

HeartLee

Without faith it is impossible to please God. In fact it says in Hebrews 11:6, "*Without faith it is impossible to please Him, for he who comes to God must believe that He is, and that He is a rewarder of those who diligently seek Him.*"

You may be on the very top of the mountain or in the lowest valley. Just know, God will never leave your side. I am reminded of two people in the Bible with great faith during difficult times.

First, when Abraham was told by God to take his dear son Isaac to the land of Moriah and sacrifice him. Abraham could not comprehend why God would tell him to do such an act. This was his promised son whom he deeply loved. When Abraham arrived at the place where God had sent him, he told his two young servants, "Stay here with the donkey. The boy and I are going over there to worship, then we'll come back to you." Wow! What faith! "...then we'll come back to you." Abraham trusted God so fully that he must have believed if he did kill his son that God would bring him back to life.

And then there was Martha. Her brother Lazarus, one of Jesus' best friends, had died and been in the grave for four days. When Jesus finally arrived Martha, a little put out, says to Jesus, "Lord if You had been here, my brother would not have died. But even now I know that whatever You ask of God, God will give You." Omgoodness! "But even now!!!" What great faith!

How encouraging it is to know that we can fully trust God with the outcome of our situation. Even if we do not understand it. Even if it looks hopeless. Even if it's dead. God has it all figured out. So, we do not have to worry.

Isaiah 43:19 says, *God will make a way where there seems to be no way.* Hosea 2:15 says, "*God is the only one who can make the valley of trouble...a door of hope.*"

it dawned on me...

I believe in divine appointments. God sends people in your life for a reason.

One of my favorite movies of all times is *The Wizard of Oz*. It is such an inspirational film about a young girl trying to find her way back home with the help of some interesting companions she meets along the way. After watching the movie as a young girl, I would daydream about a beautiful home somewhere over the rainbow.

Now that I am older, I believe there are some biblical truths hidden with spiritual messages. Like the yellow brick road, for example, many have found themselves on a path of enlightenment. It is long and often winds through treacherous places exposing us to complicated obstacles. With the help of friends like the scarecrow, tinman, and lion, we can do a little self-refection.

Meredith and HeartLee

Just like the scarecrow, we all need wisdom. James 3:17 says, "*The wisdom that is from above is first pure, then peaceable, gentle, and easy to be intreated, full of mercy and good fruits, without partiality, and without hypocrisy.*" The tinman wanted a heart that was filled with compassion. Ephesians 4:30 teaches us to be kind and compassionate to one another, forgiving others, just as in Christ God forgave you.

The lion filled with fear desired courage. Deuteronomy 31:6 says, "*Be strong and courageous. Do not be discouraged, for the Lord your God will be with you wherever you go.*" Just like that, in a heartbeat, in a flash, my life was changed. I found myself on an unknown path, surrounded by all these little people, who were my new students. Although my life had taken a detour and I felt God had forgotten me, my students saw a national heroine of hope in me. On days I could not find my way, God sent new teachers and friends to assist in my difficulties. They provided guidance, inspiration, and a new perspective.

I am now beginning to realize just how much they have touched me and how God has used them to help transform my life. 1 Corinthians 2:19 says, "*No eye has seen, no ear has heard, no mind has conceived what God has prepared for those who love Him.*" At first, finding my way back home was of utmost importance. Trying to stay on the straight and narrow path was crucial. But through the courageous efforts of my rescuers and by the sure Grace of God, I am really feeling like I am just passing through. This life is not my home, but my heart is forever filled with a colorful, rainbow smile!

Remember, often, His call is to follow paths we would not have chosen. God does not always give you the people you want. He gives you the people you need to help you, to hurt you, to leave you, to love you, and to make you into the person you are meant to be! I realize that somewhere over the rainbow, little blue birds fly. But even greater than this.... someday so will I. Psalm 27:13 says, "*We look forward to our heavenly home.*" Click – Click – click... There's no place like home!

it dawned on me...

That social media can be a good thing and a not so good thing. On a good note, social media has given me an opportunity not only to post pictures and videos of family and friends but offers a safe place to store my life's albums, so to speak.

It has also opened doors to share Christ with others by posting devotions, verses, and inspirational saying and songs. It also enables family members and friends to keep in touch from afar and reconnect with old friends. I am so thankful to have had the opportunity to reconnect with some of my military friends that I had as a young girl.

Though there are many positive facets of social media, there are some unfortunate impacts. Some negative effects on people and users are both physical and mental, such as depression and anxiety, cyberbullying, general addiction, unhealthy sleep patterns, and relationship problems. We must be cautious as to who we connect with and why we are connecting with them, and what posts we are "liking". Others may be watching and notice what we do, say, and 'like' on social media and who we are connecting with also.

As Christians, it is important we use social media as a moral and righteous tool rather than a means of immoral acts or wrong doings. Sadly, many families have been destroyed through disloyal connections on social media. In an age where we are more connected than ever through technology, many feel lonely. Maybe it is because their heart longs for a deeper connection. Life's best connections happen in person.

While digital communities like texting, Facebook, Instagram etc. can enrich our lives, they cannot replace the joy of eye contact, laughter and tears, hugging, love and affection of a live human friend. There's beauty in a simple touch, a tangible connection that binds our skin and braids our soul.

There is just something about spending time with others and hearing their hearts. Similarly, our Heavenly Father finds pleasure when you and I walk and talk with Him. He enjoys taking our hand and sharing our time, trials, treasures, and thoughts. Micah 6:8 says, "*He has shown you what is good. And what does the Lord require of you? To act justly, love mercy and walk humbly with your God.*" He longs for you and me to live in constant communion with Him. To lace our fingers with His in good, bad, scary, and sad times.

PresLee and HeartLee

it dawned on me...

That the mountain top is not meant to teach us anything. It is meant to make us something. Recently, my daughters and I visited a state park with hiking, mountain biking trails and beautiful waterfalls. I wore flip flops so that it would be easy to get in and out of the water. What I did not realize is how difficult it would be to climb up the mountain to reach the trails again. My shoes were so slippery, that I could not get a good grip and climb upward. Not only was it embarrassing, that I kept slipping and sliding on the tree roots and rocks, it was painful too.

My daughters had already reached the top and were rooting me on. I knew in order to make it up to the top, I would need to remove my flip flops, however, I knew this could be painful.

PresLee and HeartLee

Mountains, great or small, have always been wrapped with mystery. Everybody wants to reach the highest peak. I have learned that there is really no growth on top of a mountain. It's in the climb where God grows us. Psalm 18:33 says, "*He makes my feet like hinds' feet and sets me upon my high places.*" A hind is a small deer whose feet are specifically designed to navigate mountains.

In a similar way, the Lord has equipped every believer with spiritual feet that are perfectly suited for enduring the upward mountain battle in His presence and in His purpose. There will be struggles, discomfort, and uncertainties...but the outcome will be worth it!

Climbing with God always stretches our faith. When we cannot clearly see our way, we must trust Him to guide us. We must not look down at our feet but keep our eyes up and focused on Him. I love how Psalm 121:1 says, "*I will lift my eyes to the hills. Where does my help come from? My help comes from the Lord, the maker of heaven and earth. He will not let my foot slip-He who watches over me does not sleep!*" I realized that after taking my flip flops off and keeping my eyes up, I was able to get a good grip with my feet and make it up to the top.

No matter what mountain you face God provides "*His Word to light our path one step at a time.*" Psalm 119:105 God is our encourager and He will pick us up when we stumble and provide strength in times of weakness. Just keep pushing on. No rush, but when you get there...The mountain top is "crowned" with Gods glory!

it dawned on me...

There is magic in misery! What? Believe it or not, your misery can be your ministry. When I was a little girl, I was so afraid of the dark. I honestly hated bedtime and did everything possible to stay up late with my parents. I did not believe in monsters, but I just knew there was one under my bed or in my closet. I would check triple time before jumping in with my favorite stuffed animal named Fuzzy Wuzzy, who by the way, was a little freakish itself.

I had a little peace just knowing that my parents were in the room right beside me and I could call out to Mom or Dad at any second and they would come running. My mom would always reassure me that I did not need to be afraid or worried and that she loved me very much. She would encourage me to pray when I sensed a monster nearby.

This is a perfect example of how much our Heavenly Father loves us. The one who holds the whole world has no trouble holding His children and loving them completely. Praying reminds us that it does not matter how big our Monster is, our God is bigger! The issue that has caused you the most pain and difficulty prevails you to destiny. After all, no pain – no gain. Right? You need a mess to get a message. You need affliction to get a miracle.

The problem is many do not want the messes or the afflictions in life. My sweet friend, Rhoda Faye Diehl once said, "When the enemy comes messin', there's always a blessin'." I love this!

Instead of saying, "why me?" We should ask, "Why not me?" Job 11:16 says, "*Because you will forget your misery, and remember it as waters that pass away.*" We should try to remain thankful when going through a trial because deep down it could be much more devastating. In fact, I have learned to say..." Lord, thank you for this because this could be so much worse. Please teach me what I need to learn from this experience."

Though as difficult as it may seem, consider it an opportunity for great joy. For you know that when your faith is tested, your endurance has a chance to grow. When facing your monsters, just know that God can handle anything; just lay it at your Father's feet. There is nothing too big. He is the One who is large and in charge.

When your life looks like a fog, trust the God who can see right through it. He is the One who can see in the dark when we see nothing. He is the God who knows what path we should take and has promised He will get us there. When we are unsure, we can rest in the fact that He is always certain. James 1:2-4 says, "*So, let it grow, for when your endurance is fully developed, you will be perfect and complete, needing nothing.*" Through these painful and difficult experiences, we can have a greater depth of love and compassion for others. And we are also able to experience first-hand the joy and satisfaction of being able to say with all sincerity, "I understand what you're going through, and I am praying for you!"

So, tonight when you go to bed, wrap yourself up in God's blanket of peace. Philippians 4:19 says, "*My God will supply all my needs according to the riches of His glory in Christ Jesus.*" And no matter what the outcome, the good, the bad, or the ugly, God is very near. In fact, just call out, "Jesus!" And He will come running because He is your loving dad. He will pick you up and reassure you that there is no reason to be afraid or worried and that He loves you very much.

it dawned on me...

Mahayla Nicole Brewster

I felt a heart-drop! A heart-drop is when a person gives you a peek into their heart. It maybe through actual words or you may pick up on a feeling such as sadness or loneliness. Many long for someone to understand, for someone to say, "I'm listening, I hear you".

God often uses people to hear the cries of others and respond with love and care. Lamentations 2:18 says, "*God hears our heart-cries: the hearts of the people cry out to the Lord.*" God knows our pain and has access to our deepest longings. He observes our desire to be noticed and loved. And He holds every drop in His hand.

May we become skilled at tuning our ears to the heart-drops of those all around us. Hearing a heart-drop is an art we must lovingly cultivate. We can make a difference in the lives of those around us. It only takes a drop. Just a teeny, tiny drop of love. Just a small drip of compassion.

Proverbs 15:1 says, "*A gentle answer turns away wrath, but hard words stir up anger.*" You see, Proverbs 15:4 says, "*Gentle words bring life and health.*" Proverbs 18:20 also reminds us that, "*Words satisfy the soul as food satisfies the stomach, the right words on a person's lips bring satisfaction.*"

Be the drop that freely falls and becomes one with water. You might not be able to perceive the ripples you have created right away, but water will allow you to feel how their love comes back to you again and again.

We may not know what our neighbor is going through, what our co-worker is dealing with, or how the stranger we just walked by really feels. What if we dripped a smile here, and dropped a kind word there? What if we dripped a prayer for the outcast and dropped helping hands for the homeless? What if we dripped forgiveness on our betrayer, and dropped an "I'm sorry" on the guilty?

Drip, drop, drip, drop, drip, drop. Love, compassion, love, compassion, love, compassion. Just a tiny drop of your love and compassion drips from your heart, enters the water and becomes the mighty, the boundless… ocean. "It's impossible", said pride. "It's risky" said experience. "It's pointless", said reason. "Give it a try", whispered the heart." Just one drop of your love fills my heart to overflowing. You made a difference in me!

it dawned on me...

It'll be worth the wait! When I was little, I can remember turning the glass ketchup bottle upside down and just waiting and waiting and waiting for it to come out and plop on top of my fries. I would hit the bottom of the bottle over and over, but it simply just took its time....no hurry! Taught me patience, I guess.

Now days they have a squeeze bottle! Seriously??? I can still hear the ketchup commercial song they used to play. Anticipation, anticipation, it's making me wait...It's SLOOOOOW GOOOOOD!

Reminds me, that delays show us that we are not in control! Something or someone else is calling the shots. If we are sensitive to God's instruction, then each delay has a lesson. He wants to teach us patience and increase our faith. He is more interested in teaching Godly character than He is in making sure our schedule runs according to our plans. We wait on the Lord because we have the ultimate trust in His plan for our lives. It can be tough to wait on His timing, but it is always worth it!

I would rather wait on God with anticipation in my heart, then do things my way - A quick result that leads to a dead end.

Lamentations 3:25 says, "*The Lord is good to those who wait hopefully and expectantly for Him, to those who seek Him.*"

it dawned on me...

When we mess up, we should 'fess up. This applies to our relationships with other people and with God. Ephesians 4:26 says, "*Be angry, and sin not: let not the sun go down upon your wrath.*" This verse is saying, when we have wronged or offended another person, we should make it right before we go to sleep at night. I have a sense of regret in my life for not adhering to this verse sooner.

Like many, If I could relive my life, I would definitely change many things. Though we can't change the past we can attempt to make things right in the present, 1 Peter 4:4 says, "*Blessed are the peacemakers, for they shall be called sons of God.*" If we are truly sorry, we will do our best to fix it.

Even if it's not our fault, it's our responsibility to address the situation and do whatever possible to make amends. Failing to accept responsibility for sin in our lives and intentionally damaging others, precludes us from experiencing the new beginning we desperately desire.

photo by Cole Sanders

The same is true when we have sinned against God. We should make every effort to be sure things are right with Him. Receiving God's forgiveness is not a complicated process. It is probably less complicated, in fact, then making things right with people. Saying "I am sorry" is not always easy but saying "I am sorry" does a heart good. And many times, forgiving others is easier than forgiving ourselves.

The good news is that we serve a God of second chances. Praise the Lord! So even if we have messed up, God can still turn it around. Hopefully, we can fail forward, which means learning from our mistakes. 'Fessing up to our messing up is not easy but is so good for the soul. Always remember, actions speak louder than words.

it dawned on me...

That trials are the raw materials out of which God weaves His miracles. Psalm 45:11, 14 says, "*So shall the king greatly desire thy beauty, (when thou art clothed) in raiment of needlework.*" Back in the day my mother and I learned to crochet, and we would spend hours making big afghans. It was fun looping yarn with a hooked needle and making different patterns. We ended up venturing out and making potholders, decorative socks for my daughters, and even barefoot sandals, which were my fav, by the way.

Every now and then after working many hours, the strings would get pulled or caught and begin to unravel. Boy, that was disheartening, but we would just have to start again and hope for the best. This reminds me that we should not be surprised when tribulation comes, for the Bible says that the raiment we shall wear when we meet the Lord require much intricate needlework here below. When trials and sorrows are rightly received, they result in heavenly compensations. These rewards for faithful endurance far outweigh the passing pains of our earthly pilgrimage.

I find it quite interesting that a crushed rose gives off the sweetest fragrance and that the pains of childbirth are compensated by the joys of motherhood. A grain of sand makes a wound in the body of an oyster, and yet from that irritation a lovely pearl is formed. How amazing!

When my dad returned from Vietnam when I was 5 years old, he gave me a pearl ring. At the time I did not understand that this hard, glistening object on my little finger was formed within the soft tissue of a living shelled oyster mollusk. Indeed, many of the beauties of heaven will be fashioned from the bruises of earth.

When it seems your life is unraveling, so to speak, look to the One who holds all things together. Colossians 1:16-17 says, "*For in Him all things were created: things in heaven and on earth, visible and invisible, whether thrones or powers or rulers or authorities. All things have been created through Him and for Him. He is before all things, and in Him all things hold together.*" I call this the laminin verse. Laminin is a cell adhesion molecule that holds the membranes of our bodies together. If you have time, watch the YouTube video about Laminin. It is about God's love, Jesus, and laminin. It is an amazing and moving sermon that depicts the structure of the molecule, laminin.

Psalm 139:14 says, "*We are fearfully and wonderful made.*" He knows all the details of our lives. Such details as shaping the glue that holds us together in the form of a cross. Our most frayed and frazzled moments can serve as a launching pad to propel us to our faithful and unfaltering Father. Jesus died a horrible death on a cross to set us free from sin and to give us an eternal life. Our worst days should drive us to call upon our... best Hope!

Psalm 61:2 says, "*You are the One I will call when pushed to the edge*". I hope you know Jesus and have experienced His love. If not, Jesus loves you. He knows everything about you. In Him, all things hold together! So, weary sufferer, do not be dismayed by the needle pricks of pain and darkness. Think only of the joy of your King when you appear before Him in the fine needlework of the beauty of holiness!

it dawned on me...

We all have those days when we just do not understand. And it really hurts. Hurts to the core! Why God? How could you allow this to happen? Where are you God?

I am completely amazed at how Job dealt with his pain. In the course of one day, Job receives four messages, each bearing separate news that his livestock, servants, and ten children have all died due to marauding invaders or natural catastrophes. He tears his clothes and shaves his head in mourning, but he still blesses God in his prayers.

He is then afflicted with horrible skin sores and his wife encourages him to curse God, give up, and die. But Job says, "Should we accept good from God, and not bad?" In all his agony, Job did not give up or sin. I find it compelling, that "*After Job had prayed for his friends the Lord restored his prosperity and doubled his possession.*" This is found in Job 42:10. He got double for his trouble! Wow!

Job managed to stop focusing on his pain, continued to worship God, and prayed for others. How amazing that Job in all his unrelenting pain and anguish, humbly and whole-heartedly, still worshipped the Lord! Interestingly, he was the first in scripture to ever call God his Redeemer. Job 19:16 He said, "*For I know my Redeemer lives.*"

The very same God that spins things in orbit, runs to the weary, worn, and weak, and the same gentle hands that hold me when I am broken, conquered death to bring me victory! "I know my Redeemer lives!" We may not understand, but God gives peace which passes all understanding.

So, praise God in your pain, pray for others, and He will turn your sorrow into dancing and your despair into joy. As sensitive as you may feel, just allow God to shine light into your darkness, speak gladness into your mourning, bring beauty to your ashes and redeem your life from the dark pit of broken.

it dawned on me...

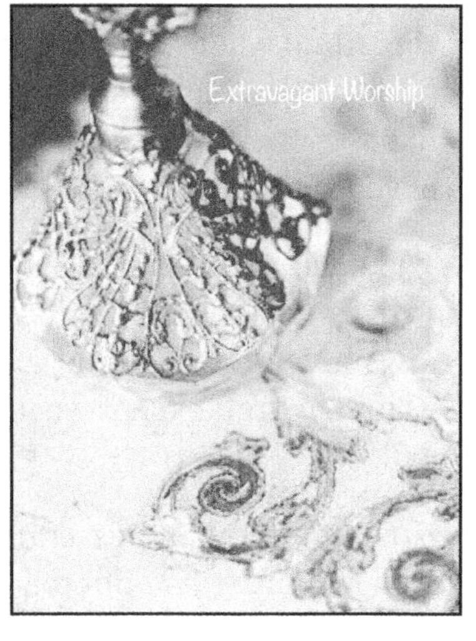

I finally get why Jesus was so happy with Mary. (I was once was a huge Martha fan.) Mary poured out her life for His glory! John 12:3 says, "*Mary took the expensive perfume and poured it on Jesus' feet. Following the same path as her perfume, her long, dark hair spilled across His feet, as Mary of Bethany, wiped His feet with her hair.*"

She was quietly letting go of self. She laid her whole being before Him: her pride, her reputation, her social standing, her clean hands, her pure heart. "*And the house was filled with the fragrance of the perfume.*" John 12:3 "*Her perfume was worth a year's wages.*" (about $30,000 today) John 12:5

I am in awe of her sacrifice. Mary did what she could. Mark 14:8 Jesus knew exactly what she could do and expected no more…no less. If only I could be so single hearted and live for an audience of just – one. If only I could be so deeply connected with this one man – Jesus. If only I can be an extravagant worshipper of God.

The extravagant heart asks how much it can give; not how little it can give. Like Mary, I want to live my life at His feet, hearing and responding to His Word.

it dawned on me...

Be careful what you partake! One of my sweet students made a comment today. I thought it most intriguing. She said, "Vanilla flavoring smells like the tears of Jesus, but tastes like the sweat of Satan". Hmmm...I never thought of it quite like that. But it sure does teach a great lesson.

The devil portrays himself as the very opposite thing of what he really is. This reminds me of the story of Adam and Eve in the Bible. God had given them the beautiful garden of Eden and told them that they could eat of any fruit except what grows on the tree of knowledge of good and evil.

Now, the serpent was craftier than any of the wild animals the Lord God had made and offered the fruit from the tree of knowledge to Eve. The snake told her that if she would partake, she would be as wise and powerful as God. The fruit did look appealing, so Eve took a bite and

gave some to Adam. The minute they ate from the forbidden tree shame, guilt, and condemnation set in as a result of committing their first sin against God.

Sometimes Satan makes things in life look beautiful and smell flavorful. He does his best to lure us into taking just one little taste. And when we give in, we find a somewhat sickening and bitter aftertaste. The closer we engage with God, the more we can know His goodness. In Psalm 34:8 He urges… "*taste and see that I am good.*" God's goodness is what He wants us to experience.

it dawned on me...

Car crashes through house

We are not defined by the storms in our lives. We are defined by the Savior Who is in the middle of the storm. The truth about the storms of life is that sometimes survival is not pretty. Many times, the storms knock us down and we feel as if our lives are completely over!

No matter what you are facing, a betrayal, a loss of a loved one, a not-so-good doctor's report, loss of a job or possible foreclosure. No matter what your storm may be, it is not bigger than God and it is not a surprise to Him either. He knows the beginning to the end. He sees the whole picture and even knows the ending.

Many of you may be right in the middle of a pandemic. It is important to lean into God and allow Him to pick you up and help you get back on your feet again. Sometimes storms are a means of transportation. 2 Corinthians 12:10 says, "*I delight in weaknesses, in insults, in hardships, in persecutions, in difficulties. For when I am weak, then I am strong.*"

Do not get stuck! Get up and move! If you keep on moving, you will get through it. Anything in your life right now that seems too big is just a shadow. And God is bigger than your shadow! Psalm 23:4 says, "*Though I walk through the valley of the shadow of death, I will fear no evil for Thou art with me.*" When you cannot walk another step, God will carry you. I promise you will never walk it alone! Our God is still good, even when things are bad.

it dawned on me...

Journey Church

Sometimes I get a little tired of the mystery of it all. Knowing in my heart that God is working behind the scenes but having to believe and not see is frustrating at times. When life seems to only give lemons and we have shaken off every reasoning and can find no reason.

Does God really care? Where is He anyway? Sometimes we are tempted to believe our Father has forsaken us. "My God, my God, why hast thou forsaken me?" Jesus spoke these words. And these words assure us of every struggle, every valley, every circumstance being vindicated, corrected and justified on the cross. These are the words of our own heart at times.

Yes, God does care, and He has never left our side. He is working behind the scenes even when we cannot see Him, He is working. Even when we cannot feel Him, He is working. He never gets weary or tired. He never sleeps. How comforting this is to know. In Romans 8:28 Paul says, "*And we know that all things work together for good to those who love God, to those who are called according to His purpose.*"

We do not have to try and figure it all out. God already knows the ending. His ways are higher than ours. It is not important that we understand everything but that we trust God in the process. The process may hurt for a little while, but joy will come in the morning. Sometimes there is great mourning until a new morning arises. Rest tonight in the fact that our God is a good Father and He is for us. His plans are far greater than anything we can imagine or dream of. The mystery of it all will begin to unravel at just the right time. Hold on to His promises and do not give up. His purpose is greater than our problems and our pain. Every storm is a school. Every trial is a teacher. Every experience is an education. Every difficulty is for our development.

So, let God unravel the perfect plan. Until then, let God grow you into the person He wants you to be.

it dawned on me...

Precisely what David meant when he wrote, "*Thou anointest my head with oil.*" From Psalm 23.

A good shepherd would always wipe oil all over the face of his sheep to prevent flies from entering their nasal passages. If the oil were not applied, flies could deposit eggs in the mucus membranes of the sheep's nose. When the eggs hatch, they would make their way up in the sheep's head, burrowing into their flesh, causing intense irritation. For relief, a sheep would deliberately bang its head on trees, rocks, and posts in efforts to ease the pain by killing themselves.

If just one sheep goes astray, the gentle shepherd searches after the lost sheep until he finds it. And when he finds his lost lamb, he then joyfully puts it on his shoulders and calls his friends and neighbors and says, "Rejoice with me because I found my lost sheep."

God is our good Shepherd and we are His sheep. Our Shepherd is alert to every disaster that threatens His sheep. No matter what storm we face or what giant we come against, our good Shepherd is our protector. He fights for us when we cannot fight for ourselves. I tell you there will be rejoicing in heaven over one sinner who repents than over ninety- nine who do not.

To make it personal, He saw me, this lost sheep, this broken vessel with regret as deep as the ocean. This sinner had wandered so far away, and my mistakes pained His heart deeply. Yet, He found me, and He put me on His shoulders, and He carried me home.

In Psalm 23, the Psalmist tells us that the Lord is our shepherd and He protects His flock from evil. Sheep need leadership. Without it, they wander off and are injured or killed. Isaiah explains that we "all like sheep, have gone astray, each of us has turned to our own way".

I read a story once about shepherds in ancient Israel breaking the leg of a sheep who wanders. While the leg is healing, it is said that the sheep would become endeared to the shepherd as he nurtures them back to health, carrying the disabled sheep close to his heart.

Like sheep, we are totally dependent on the good Shepherd to provide our sustenance. He is attentive to our needs. When we enter the flock of the good shepherd, His very words feed our soul and His Spirit quenches our thirst. God is our Chief Shepherd. Psalm 23 tells us that "He guides me along the right paths for His name's sake." When we keep our eyes on Him, we do not need to look to the left or the right. We simply need to follow Him.

Jesus the good Shepherd is just as much a corrector as He is a comforter. Sometimes He will block the things we want and lead us to the things we need! Today, if He is your Chief Shepherd, your security is not in your situation. Your security is in your Savior. You are secure in Jesus!

it dawned on me...

That every rose has its thorn. Harriet Beecher Stowe once said that gardeners, when they would bring a rose to rich flowering, deprive it for a season of light and moisture. Silent and dark it stands, dropping one faded leaf after another until it looks dead. But when the plant stands stripped to the uttermost, a new life is even then working in the buds from which shall spring a tender foliage and a brighter wealth of flowers.

I can personally testify to the truth of her words. Suddenly I was robbed of happiness and felt sorely afflicted and in dire distress. As I stood there, stripped from everything I had known, I didn't know what to do or where to go. I was left physically and mentally crippled, and in some ways handicapped.

My world had fallen apart, my family broken, and the pain unbearable. Through many agonizing days and nights, the suffering ravaged my frail body. I knew deep down that God was near and had something extremely important to teach me, but I felt utterly forsaken.

"Why am I going through such terrible trials? Why do my prayers for deliverance go unanswered? Doesn't God care that I'm suffering so much?" Does this sound familiar? Everyone has a story.

I remember many situations that Joseph encountered as he was growing up. As a boy he was full of dreams about his foreshadowed greatness. A starry-eyed idealist, he seemed to lack the strength and force of character necessary to rule. His brothers plotted to kill him, and he was left to die in a pit, then sold into slavery. He ended up in prison for a crime that he did not commit. Imprisonment, however, appeared to have changed him. When he was released, he acted like a born ruler of men, displaying wisdom, modesty, courage, and firm resolution. He trusted God completely.

By Joseph's own testimony, the sufferings – physical, mental, and emotional agonies – had been allowed by God so that Joseph could fulfill God's plan; to save many lives. " *But as for you* (Joseph's brothers who had sold him into slavery many years previously), *ye thought evil against me; but God meant it unto good, to bring to pass, as it is this day, to save much people alive.*" Genesis 50:20 God was also pleased with the ancient patriarch, Job. For he had shown himself faithful through all his trials.

Often today when the Lord's people are afflicted, it is because He would exhibit them as outstanding trophies of His grace before the world and Satan. Do not disappoint the Savior, then, by being rebellious! Rather, testify with Job, "Though He slay me, yet will I trust in Him!"

So, in the storms of life God sometimes intervenes on our behalf and shelters us, while at other times He allows us to be exposed so that we will be pressed more closely to Him. Though as difficult as it may seem, we as Christians should honor the Lord's expectation by praising rather than complaining. God sends trials to improve us, not to impair us. Psalm 119:71 says, "*It is good for me that I have been afflicted, that I might learn thy statutes.*"

Through my trials I learned of Jesus' love, and today I have a deep, satisfying joy and peace. God will lead you just as faithfully if you will let Him. After the winds of betrayal or disappointments hit and only devastation is left, we will grieve. But remember grieving is a bridge we must cross in order to embrace relief. Psalm 34:18 says, "*The Lord is close to the brokenhearted and saves those who are crushed in spirit.*" We must trust God to bring out the good in it all. "We grieve with hope." 1 Thessalonians 4:13 When God puts a tear in your eye, it is because He wants to put a rainbow in your heart.

it dawned on me...

Heartlee and Preslee

It would be amazing to be a superhero and possess superhuman strength. When my brothers were little, they could not wait to watch Batman and Robin zoom out of the Batcave driving the heavily armored tactical assault vehicle called the Batmobile. This Dynamic Duo would always come to the aid to defend Gotham City.

For some reason I always wanted to be Batgirl, putting on a helmet and speeding down the street on my motorcycle. I am sure my brothers would both have enjoyed being given the strength and ability to fly like Superman or the speed and agility of Spiderman. But I would prefer Wonder woman, not only for the costume, but for her hair. But for now, I will be content to just be Supermom!

Keeping my eyes focused on my daughters through X-Ray vision, doctoring scrapes, cuts, and broken hearts, are only a few of my superpowers. Not to mention, my problem solving and multitasking skills. But most of all my everlasting love. I remember playing Barbies when I was a little girl. I had a great set up of houses, cars, tents, pools, and more. Either my older brother Danny brought his G.I. Joe's, armed with weapons and equipment ready to fire, or my little brother David, would have his creature from the black lagoon creeping in the homes of my dolls and hiding under their beds.

Needless to say, there was never a dull moment in our household. I guess we tend to think of Superheroes when it comes to being brave, strong, and heroic. Courage has been defined as bravery too. Jesus uses the word **courage** to mean *be encouraged or take heart*. There is also moral courage which is the ability to do right in the face of opposition and discouragement. Having moral courage means that you are an honest person. It means you have integrity. Being honest and brave in such an imperfect world is not so easy. It takes an uncommon courage to stand up against some of the pressures we face.

Acts 18:9 says, "*Do not be afraid, keep on speaking, do not be silent.*" When you have Jesus, you have all the courage you need for whatever you may face. My brave may look different than yours. That is why it is so important to step out and take risks. It not only changes who we are but it changes those around us, too. If you sense God telling you to witness to a co-worker, pray with a stranger, or simply stand up for what you believe. Not only will you be blessed but someone else will be blessed too. Isaiah 55:11 says, "*So shall My word be that goes forth from My mouth; It shall not return to Me void, but it shall accomplish what I please, and it shall prosper in the thing for which I sent it.*" It also says in Ephesians 6:10 "*Finally, be strong in the Lord and in the strength of His might.*" Do not let the Caped Crusaders receive all the glory because Luke 10:19 says, "*Behold, I have given you authority to tread on serpents and scorpions, and over all the power of the enemy, and nothing shall hurt you.*"

Wow! With God nothing is impossible! Today I want to encourage you to "Be strong and courageous. Do not be afraid or discouraged for the Lord your God, is with you wherever you go!" Joshua 1:9 So, superheroes do not only come dressed in a mask and cape. Sometimes they look like you and me. Be someone's hero today and help make the world a better place.

it dawned on me...

That I am intrigued by amazing magic acts and illusions. Back in the olden days we were amazed just to see the magician pull a rabbit out of his hat and see a woman being sawed in half. But today, magicians appear to defy gravity by making an object, a person, or themselves float in the air. Levitation…Wow!

The word magic is believed to have supernatural power over natural forces. I find it interesting that the word **abracadabra** means – "I create what I speak." Oh, how damaging our words can be sometimes. Sticks and stones most certainly break my bones and words hurt even worse!

What is really behind those big luscious lips anyway? Do not be fooled by that handsome smile or those pink glossy lip smackers. What the tongue says is more important. So, tame your tongue! In James it says that "The tongue is such a small part of the body, but it can make great boasts." So, it is extremely important to think before we speak. A word out of your mouth may seem of no account, but it can accomplish nearly anything – or destroy it.

As a child, I remember having a big Smokey the Bear book and I loved reading it to my little brother. I read that it only takes a spark to set off forest fires. How amazing that only one teeny, tiny spark could do such tremendous damage.

My brother would cry when we would get to the pictures of the poor animals that were trapped from the senseless flames. But even more interesting is how the Bible compares forest fires to the tongue. How great a forest is set ablaze by such a small fire! The tongue is also a fire, a world of evil among the parts of the body. Proverbs 13:3 says, "*Out of the same mouth comes goodness and praise, evil and cursing. Be careful what you say and protect your life.*" A careless talker destroys himself. Proverbs 15:4 says, "*A gentle tongue is a tree of life, but perverseness in it breaks the spirit.*" If this world throws hate at us, we can speak love back at it. If everything in the world is going the other way; we can speak God's way right back at it. Oh, how a gentle tongue is a tree of life! Such good fruit falls from it. It says in Proverbs that "*A gentle answer will calm a person's anger, but an unkind answer will cause more anger.*" In other words, if you do not have anything nice to say, do not say anything at all. Remember that kindness is contagious!

Psalm 19:14, one of my favorite verses, says, "*May the words of my mouth and the meditation of my heart be pleasing to You, O Lord, my rock and my redeemer.*" Proverbs 15:28 says, "*The heart of the righteous weighs its answers, but the mouth of the wicked gushes evil.*" It is sad when one must paint a dark picture of another in order to paint a perfect picture of themselves. SOOO, Abracadabra...POOF! Speak life!

it dawned on me...

What Romans 8:31 really means. "*God is so evidently for us, that nothing or no one can successfully be against us!*" Just a reassuring verse to remember right smack in the middle of the madness. I'll never forget some of my daughter's friends rolling our house one night. She had to be somewhere at 5:00 the next morning so when I walked her out the front door to her car, we saw what looked like freshly fallen snow. Kids will be kids and PresLee absolutely loved it.

Me, not so happy. I had the flu and was sicker than I had ever been it seemed. My thought was to just leave it like it was and clean it up later. The problem with that was, bad weather was coming in and the wind had already started blowing the snow into my neighbor's yard. I did not want them to wake up and see the mess in their front lawn.

Also my neighbors down the road knew I was sick, and I was afraid they would try and clean up the whole mess while I went back to sleep. So, I began raking up the snow. My mind was racing, and I began thinking about how much I admired Paul in the Bible. Paul was one of the most influential leaders of the early Christian church. He played a crucial role in spreading the gospel and wrote much of the New Testament while he was in prison. He suffered greatly, was persecuted, locked in chains and just waiting to die there. But he had this conviction whether he was in prison or a palace, that God is able!

Ephesians 3:20 says, "*Now to Him, who is able to do immeasurably more than all we ask or imagine according to His power that is at work within us.*" There is nothing that God can't do. When our plans become paralyzed, circumstances seem chaotic, and our future looks frail. When people seem passionless. When words are reckless, look to God's handiwork in all the havoc. If it is not fabulous, God is not finished! God views every mess as a message. "*Be patient, God is not finished with you yet!*" Philippians 1:6

it dawned on me...

It takes a lot of work resuscitating something that God is trying to terminate. There were many occasions in my life when I held on to things that God did not intend for me to have. It was like a game of tug of war. I would pull and pull and pull on the rope, but it would not budge. At the time I felt total rejection but since have learned it was God's protection.

Do not let what breaks your heart, destroy your life. Sometimes it may seem that evil prevails, and that God has looked the other way. Does He even care? Why would He allow this? How could He let them treat me this way? Do you even see us down here? It is difficult to untangle all the emotions wrapped in and around these questions. But many times, God is steering us in a new direction. Sometimes God uses our darkest moments, and the darkest people to change our hearts forever, for the better.

Sometimes we find ourselves at the intersection of our lives and something comes along and knocks us to our knees and makes us doubt. It is not the haters, it is not enemies, it is not backbiters, it is not liars that are the battlefield. The real battleground is in our head. We should not waste our weapons on what people say because it is not what they say that matters, it is what you say about you that threatens your destiny.

You will never be defeated by what they say about you. You will be defeated by what you say about you. We cannot let the rumors and the stain about what people have said destroy our opportunities. If you can kill it in your head, then you can kill it in your life. If it is still living in your head, it is still living in your life. We should say, "Not today Satan!" Philippians 3:13 says, "*Forgetting what is behind and reaching to those things that are before me.*"

Did you know that your enemies, your competitors and your critics are a blessing in disguise? Very often your enemies will say the true things about us that your friends will not say. Our enemies, our competitors, our critics are our gift. If you ain't got haters, then you aint doin' nothin', right? Its easy to love and pray for people who love us and who are kind to us. Luke 6:27-28 says, "*But I tell you who hear me: love your enemies, do good to those who hate you, pray for those who mistreat you.*"

If we could only process things through the filter of the absolute assurance of God's love. Then we could see that God loves us so much, therefore, we must trust why He is allowing us to go through certain things. This breaking is shaping us into what God would have us to be, a new you and a stronger you. His love and face cover your exposed grief! Psalm 138:8 says, "*The Lord will fulfill His purpose in me. Your steadfast love, endures forever.*"

it dawned on me...

God's got this! Sometimes you just need to hear it from someone. "Gooooood's GOOOOOOT THIIIIIIIS!!!"

I enjoy spending time with God outdoors. Weather permitting, I put on my work boots and start walking all over my backyard in deep conversation with my Father, God. One of my favorite places to sit is on a swing hanging from a pergola covered with trailing vines in my backyard. Sometimes the vines are so long, it reminds me of a snake peeking its head out. Thankfully, I have not encountered any wild reptiles in my jungle and faithfully am believing I never will. Keeping my fingers crossed! In fact, God has been dealing with me about faith lately.

PresLee

I always pray that God will help me fuel my heart with faith and not fear. Matthew 12:20 says, Jesus said, "*Truly I tell you, if you have faith like a grain of mustard seed, you can say to this mountain, 'move from here to there,' and it will move. Nothing will be impossible for you.*" My daughter PresLee had a volleyball game the other day and our team was winning. The fans were extremely excited, and the girls were so happy and aggressive. Then suddenly, the other team made a comeback. They stepped up their game because they did not want to lose. They took the lead and I started to get frustrated and partly angry when I noticed our team's energy level dropping. It was almost as if our girls wanted to give up. This man behind me had the audacity to say, "They can still win this game. All you need is faith as small as a grain of mustard seed. They can pull this off," he added. "They've got this. They can win."

And then suddenly, it was like I found a grain! I've got a grain, I shouted inside my heart! It felt like I had a whole handful of mustard seeds! It's amazing how one person can encourage you when your faith is really low.

You know, faith makes things possible, not easy. Joshua 1:9 says, "*Be strong and courageous. Do not be afraid; or discouraged, for the Lord your God is with you wherever you go.*" If you happen to be someone who is walking in the valley of the shadow of death, the lowest possible place that you can be in this life, just know that God will carry you through. He will never leave you. Corinthians 12:9 says, "*My grace is sufficient for thee: for my strength is made perfect in weakness.*"

When life takes a wild detour and we find ourselves caught up in the vines of an imperfect world, take comfort in the fact that God's plan is always bigger and better than ours. In desperation just cry out to the Lord because He is not just near, He will get you through this. Psalm 18:31-32 says, "*For whom is God, but the Lord: And who is a rock except our God? The God who equipped me with strength and made my way blameless.*"

When you feel like giving up, you do not have to comprehend the whole entire journey. You only need enough strength to take one more step. So, I would like to encourage you by reminding you what I heard a couple of days ago at the volleyball game. There is still hope. All you need is faith. All you need is faith as small as a mustard seed. You can do this. It is possible. God's got this!

it dawned on me...

God's creation is valuable to Him. Today on my daughter, HeartLee's 19th birthday, she found a baby bird whimpering about, trying to avoid our black cat named Blu. As the tears fell down her round cheeks and her tender heart began to break, she nestled the little bird in her shirt. After trying to feed it water with a dropper, we began trying to figure out where to get a worm. We made a nest in the bottom of the clothes basket and put the little thing in a quiet warm room. After googling baby birds, we found out that it was a fledgling. We knew that its mother was probably nearby and would need to continue to teach it how to fly and take care of itself. So, we decided to take it back outside but not so close to our house. Later, Heartlee thought she saw its mother flying near where we put the little bird, and this made her smile.

You know, when I was a little girl, I remember saving a bird in my backyard after hurricane Eloise. This was one of the most destructive, tropical, cyclones of the 70's. My family found shelter in the hospital where my dad worked. For kids it was fun because it was like having a sleepover, but with hundreds of people. We got to sleep in the halls in sleeping bags and enjoy ready-to-eat meals. We had no idea the devastation that Eloise would bring. I wrapped the poor wet bird in a towel and put it in a clothes basket. I gave it water through a dropper and fed it some worms. The next day, I could not believe my eyes. There was a beautiful, blue bird in the basket, and it was trying to fly. We took it outside and the bird flew away. This made me smile.

You know, God does not forget a single bird. He sees all the little birds that fall by the wayside, and He sees you too. He will protect you, rescue you, hold you, answer you, honor you, and satisfy you." Psalm 91:9-16 says, "*Look at the birds of the air; they do not sow, or reap or store away in barns, and yet your Heavenly Father feeds them. Are you not much more valuable then they?*" Matthew 6:25-26 "*God is your refuge and your shelter.*" He will give you all you need from day today, just trust and focus on Him.

it dawned on me...

Photo by Gail Carlisle Caldwell

When faced with a dead end, expect God to act. Not too long ago my family and I found ourselves in a situation we never dreamed we would be in. In fact, it was a nightmare. It felt as if a Tsunami hit our home and none of us would survive.

It reminds me of a reoccurring nightmare I have had throughout my lifetime. In my dream I would either be with family or friends having a good time. Then suddenly, out of nowhere a huge wave appeared and began to grow, and grow, and grow until it covered the sky. We would all run for our lives in the opposite direction of the wave. It seemed as if we were trying to outrun the wave and make it to a safe place. I prayed that I would not be swallowed by the waters and hoped no one else would be either.

This reminds me of the Bible story of Jonah. In Jonah chapter 1, the Lord tells him to get up and go to the great city of Nineveh. He told Jonah to announce His judgment against it because He had seen how wicked its people were. But Jonah got up and went in the opposite direction hoping to escape from the Lord by sailing to Tarshish.

I remember praying continually for my family members. I was desperate and needed nothing less than a miracle. In my war room I remember crying out, "Lord, please change him!" You see, I was believing for a miracle, even though the situation seemed hopeless in the natural eye. In fact, many gave me their opinions about the matter. I heard comments such as, "He has his own will," "He can only change if he wants to change," and "We are not robots, God won't make us do something we don't want to do." Although I understood where they were coming from, I was a little bewildered. Why, when Jonah was sailing to Tarshish, did the Lord hurl a powerful wind over the sea, and cause a violent storm that threatened to break the ship apart. You see, Jonah knew he had done wrong and told the sailors to throw him into the raging sea. When they did, the storm stopped at once. The Lord had arranged for a great fish to swallow Jonah, And he was inside the fish for three days and three nights.

I guess you could say this got his attention. From inside the fish Jonah prayed to the Lord his God. And the Lord commanded the fish to spew Jonah onto dry land. Needless to say, Jonah obeyed the word of the Lord and went to Nineveh. I think that the key word in this story is 'arranged'. Yes, Jonah did have his own will, but God is powerful enough to arrange things in our lives to get us back on the right track. Proverbs 19:21 says, "*Many are the plans in a man's heart, but it is the Lord's purpose that prevails.*" Sometimes we do run into dead end places in our lives and we do not know where to turn or even how to pray. During these trying times we discover that in our own strength, we are no match for life's problems. When we have no words, God hears our heart. We can also allow the Holy Spirit to pray through us. God hears our prayers from the moment we humbly call upon His name. I can remember praying and asking God to give me living words, from the Bible. I held on tightly to this one, Proverbs 21:1 "*The king's heart is like a stream of water directed by the Lord; He guides it wherever He pleases.*"

It comforting to know that God can take a king's heart and turn it any which way He pleases. If He can do that for a king's heart, surely, He could do that for my family, right? As I continued to pray for many, many months that God would change his heart, I realized... that it was my heart that He changed. When the waters of life are overwhelming, or you see a dead-end sign ahead, know that God can turn a crucifixion into a resurrection, a dead end into deliverance, and graves into gardens. Praise God! He can turn things around so do not lose hope. Faith plus delays, difficulties, dead ends equal deliverance!

it dawned on me...

One of my favorite times of the year was when the circus came to town. As a little girl, I could not wait to enter the big top and be seated on the bleachers with a big bag of popcorn. I can still hear the ringmaster shout, “Ladies and gentlemen, boys and girls, children of all ages, get ready for The Greatest Show on Earth.” There would be silly clowns doing acrobatics and men juggling fire and more.

My favorite part of the circus was the flying trapeze. It was a little unnerving because the flyer must wait for a call from the catcher to make sure he or she leaves at the correct time. Otherwise, the catcher will not be close enough to the flyer to make a successful catch. I was most intrigued however, with the tight rope walker. There was utter silence inside the tent as someone walked on a thin wire or rope. And many times, they were blindfolded. I always held my breath and never made a sound. I wanted so much to walk on that tight rope myself. Immediately after the circus had ended, I went home and tied a yellow rope to two poles on my front

Hannah, Heart, Pres

porch. I enjoyed playing circus with my friends and was extremely happy to finally be the tight rope walker.

I guess my daughter, PresLee continued the tightrope tradition. One day she was babysitting, during a church service at my mom and dad's house. She was watching a few little ones in my bedroom during the service. I was telling one of the mothers how much PresLee loved children and how responsible she was at her age with them. After the service we opened the bedroom door to the woman's little one walking on a plank from one bed to another. My jaw dropped, and I had no words.

Years later, as an adult, I had to step out of my comfort zone once again. So, I opened the door and with my eyes closed, I took one step. With a simple little peek, I noticed the tightrope under my feet. Do I dare continue with fear of what the future may hold? At times, the wind blew so hard and balancing on such a thin string seemed impossible.

Do I risk it all? Do I question if God will show up? Even though I could not fathom what was ahead, I prayed with each step I took, believing this was God's plan once again. Stepping out of our comfort zones can be scary and to do it more than once takes true faith. Maybe it is time for you to step out on the tightrope of faith and trust Him in the wait. Joshua 1:9 says, "*Be strong and courageous. Do not be frightened and do not be dismayed, for the Lord, your God is with you wherever you may go.*"

If we never take a risk and trust in God to step out of our comfort zones, we will never know the fullness of the riches and blessing God has waiting for us. Do not look down and plummet to the ground. Keep your eyes focused on Him and He will safely lead the way. God may seem silent in the wait and you may not be able to breath at first. But if you keep your eyes focused on God and really listen, He will whisper in your ear, "You can do this."

It is my birthday! Loved them when I was little, not so much fun these days! #gettingolder #shouldbegrateful

I remember the good ole days so well when my mom always planned a big birthday party. We had lots of cake and ice cream, balloons, friends, and presents.

Now my girls never fail to remember my special day. Starting off our morning, HeartLee bought us McGriddle biscuits and hash browns from McDonald's. Yummy! Then she and Preslee surprised me with a very special gift. It was a record player in a pink case. Something I have always wanted. It brings back such sweet memories of my mom and I going shopping for records when I was little. I still have all my 45's and albums. I cannot wait to try them out on my new toy.

This reminds me of one of my favorite birthday presents when I was little. It was a beautiful, purple bicycle with a white basket and horn on the handlebars. I was turning 6 years old and was extremely excited to finally have a big girl bike. Boy, was I ready to ride! After my cake and ice cream, all my friends grabbed their bikes and began racing down the street. The last thing I remember is scrubbing someone's back tire and falling to the ground on my chin. Who would have thought I would spend my birthday in the hospital? Stitches....so many stitches. I still have the scar on my chin to show for it. Definitely an unforgettable birthday.

Is growing old really that bad though? Well one of the greatest benefits of getting old is the spiritual growth I have experienced. 2 Corinthians 14:6 says, "*Though our outer self is wasting away, our inner self is being renewed day by day.*" I realize that God created me to fill a special spot in His plan, a place no one else can fill. He has taught me so many lessons. Some I have caught on quickly while others I have been a slow learner.

Either way, He has been changing me and growing me into the person He wants me to be. So yes, I am grateful for another year. Birthdays now remind me of God's faithfulness. My life is full, and every day brings sweet surprises! Count your many blessings, birthday by birthday! Funny thing, not too long ago, an old friend complimented one of my pictures on Social Media. They mentioned the cute cleft in my chin. Maybe scars are not so bad after all. Evidently this one fell right into place.

it dawned on me...

That I shall not be moved. I love what Jeremiah 17:7-8 says, "*But blessed is the one who trusts in the Lord whose confidence is in Him. They will be like a tree planted by the water that sends out its roots by the stream. It does not fear when heat comes; its leaves are always green. It has no worries in a year of drought and never fails to bear fruit.*" Because it is healthy, and deeply planted, the tree is able to stand firm.

Not too long ago, my daughters and I were going through a very difficult season. Our family had been torn apart and we were forced out of our home and did not even have enough money to support ourselves. But in the midst of all this chaos, we learned the importance of maintaining a close relationship with Christ and depending solely upon Him. Never

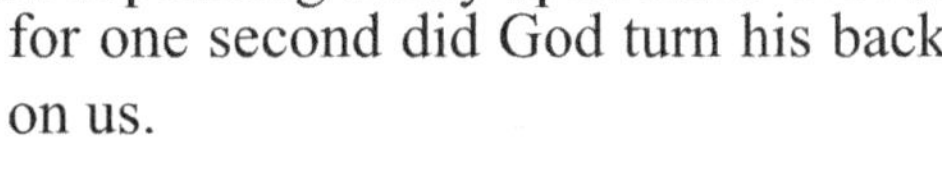

for one second did God turn his back on us.

Thanks to God and my realtor, Kristen, and after many months of prayer, God blessed me and my daughters with a beautiful home. He provided even when there seemed to be no way. I thank God every day for the many blessings He has poured in our lives. After moving in, I wanted to give my yard a facelift. I do not have a green thumb, so to speak, but I have enjoyed working in my yard. I dug twelve bushes up on my own and put down mulch. I even put a border around my flower bed and filled it with river rocks. I made a bird bath and even put solar lights all around outside. Boy, does my house light up at night.

Funny thing, on social media a friend asked for landscaping ideas because she wanted to get some yard work done, so I posted a couple of my pictures. Someone else commented that she should hire my company to do the work for her because it looked very professional. I am extremely blessed to live in such a peaceful place.

Several weeks later, I was shocked to see some weeds growing in the rocks and flower beds. It's as if the weeds were trying to strangle my flowers and the few bushes that I had left. Are you kidding me? All this hard work for this? I realized very quickly that maintenance is extremely important in order to upkeep a yard.

Reminds me, in the midst of all the challenges that seem to entangle us every day, is it even possible to live in a place of constant peace? Paul said that he found the secret of living in peace. Philippians 4:11-13 He says, "*I have learned to be content whatever the circumstances. I know what it is to be in need, and I know what it is to have plenty. I have learned the secret of being content in any and every situation, whether well fed or hungry, whether living in plenty or in want. I can do all this through Him who gives me strength.*" In other words, I have learned to live where circumstances do not move me.

So, do not be moved by the doctor's report. Do not be moved by what is in your bank account. Do not be moved by what someone did to you or said about you. Only be moved by the Word of God! God gave me this verse during my trying season and it is filled with hope, Psalm 46:5 says, "*God is in the midst of her. She shall not be moved or shaken. God shall help her at the break of dawn.*" This is so powerful! It doesn't matter what you are facing, when God is in the midst of you, there is no need to worry. Psalm 16:8, 9 also says, "*I have set the Lord always before me: because He is at my right hand, I shall not be moved. Therefore, my heart is glad, and my glory rejoiceth: my flesh also shall rest in hope.*" It is so refreshing to know that God takes care of His children and His rain will melt hard hearts and give peace to uncertain futures. Psalm 65:9-11 says, "*You take care of the earth and water it, making it rich and fertile. The river of God has plenty of water. It provides a bountiful harvest of grain for you have ordered it so. You drench the plowed ground with rain, melting the clouds and leveling the ridges. You soften the earth with showers and bless its abundant crops. You crown the year with bountiful harvest; even the hard pathways overflow with abundance.*"

God desires to reign in our lives pouring down love, peace, mercy, grace, and favor. His showers nourish new potential in our lives.

it dawned on me...

That it has been five years today that my mother gained her angel wings. It seems quite fitting that today we would celebrate my mom's mother's birthday with all our relatives at Lakepoint, Eufaula. And, by the way, many whispered in my ear how much I reminded them of my mother.

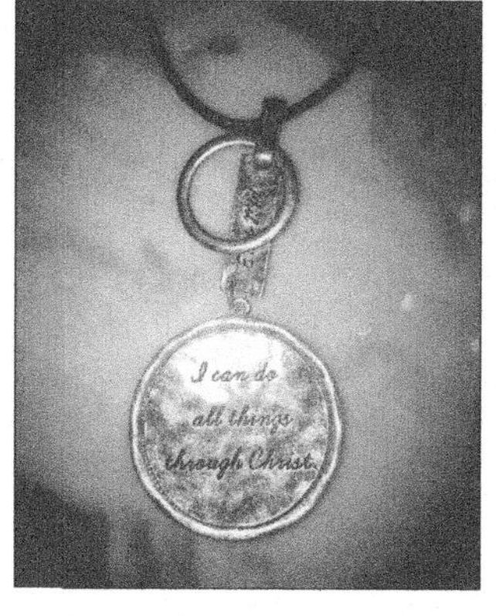

Also, my daughter HeartLee, had no idea that today was any different than any other day and presented me with a beautiful necklace. It had my mother's favorite verse on it, Philippians 4:13, "*I can do ALL things through Christ who strengthens me.*"

Isn't it amazing how God allows things to fall perfectly into place at the perfect time? My mom tucked this verse away in her heart to bring comfort as she battled a rare inflammatory disease called Transverse Myelitis. She lived many, many years with extreme pain, muscle weakness, and paralysis. But she never complained, not one time.

When Paul wrote this verse in Philippians, I believe this is what he meant and what my mother truly felt. "I can be content in any situation." Meaning - In all the twists and turns in life, we can find strength in Jesus. We can choose to wallow in self-pity, or we can allow God to turn our pity into praise.

No matter what you are going through today, you may be running on empty or simply do not have the strength to carry on. You may not have much human strength, but God can infuse you with His strength.

it dawned on me...

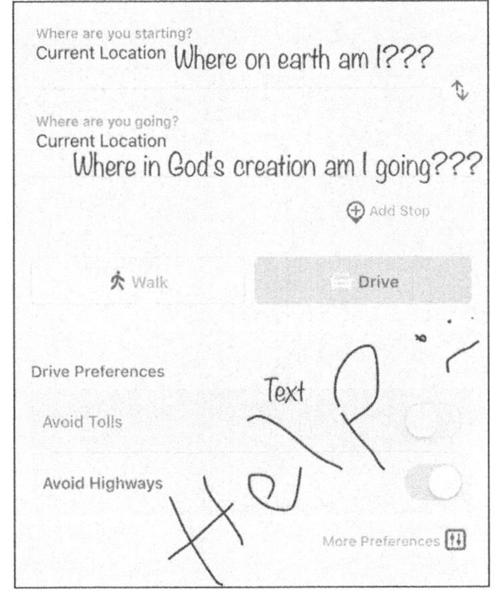

I would literally die and be left for dead on the side of the road without my Mapquest app. Moving somewhere new is like being trapped in the middle of nowhere! I am like, "God, I know You are in the middle of this but honestly, where am I, and what on earth am I doing here?" So, needless to say, I am super dependent on this helpful gadget.

My daughter PresLee played every sport in High School, so I was constantly traveling to many schools and parks during the week. The games seem to always be out in the boondocks. Before I had Mapquest I just had to ask for directions and pray I could find it. I got lost once and it was a such an unnerving feeling to drive up to a stranger's house and ask for help. Thankfully, on this particular afternoon, I knocked on the door of the sweetest family ever. They not only eased the anxiety I felt, but actually took me to the school where the game was being held. I was extremely grateful for the kindness shown to me that night.

God is always looking out for His children. Praise the Lord! Although it is comforting that Mapquest can get me pretty much anywhere I need to go, without cellular connection, it is pretty much useless. If only my faith could be so ignited in my God Quest app. Hebrews 11:1 says, "*Faith is the confidence that what we hope for will actually happen and it gives us assurance about things we cannot see.*" Who needs Wi-Fi, when you've got God-fi? God will never lead us along the wrong route or even leave us when the road gets rough. And although we may not understand why He steers us down a particular road, we should remain confident that God knows how to get us safely to our final destination!

it dawned on me...

When God shows up, He shows out! Are you facing odds that are not in your favor? Have you been given a slim chance? Your situation might look completely hopeless, but just as His hand perfectly paints all the beautiful colors in the sky for you, He will breathe into your spirit a breakthrough!

This reminds me of the story of King Jehoshaphat. He ruled 25 years in Jerusalem. At one point during his reign, some people came to start a war with Jehoshaphat. They were the Moabites, Ammonites and some Meunites. Jehoshaphat was told that a large army was coming against him. He was afraid for his people and asked the Lord what to do. All of Judah began to fast and pray. The Lord spoke and said, "Do not be afraid or discouraged because of this vast army. For the battle is not yours, but God's. Tomorrow march down against them. You will not have to fight this battle. Take up your positions; stand firm and see the deliverance the Lord will give you."

Early in the morning they set out and Jehoshaphat appointed men to sing to the Lord and to praise him for the splendor of His holiness as they went out at the head of the army. In other words, Jehoshaphat put his praise and worship team on the front lines. As they began to sing and praise, the Lord set ambushes and caused confusion against the men who were invading Judah. They basically fought and destroyed one another. Jehoshaphat and his army won the battle by standing still. When Jehoshaphat saw the armies running towards them with weapons, he had no idea what God's plan was. It must have been incredibly difficult just to stand still and trust that God knew what He was doing.

If we can just trust God in our darkest hour, everything will work out according to His perfect plan. The battle is His so never give up. You cannot lose because even in death there is victory!

So, take a leap of faith, for God is forever faithful. In Romans it says, "*Any trials that we as believers face provides an opportunity for our faith to be strengthened, and for God to be glorified because it is in our weakness that his strength and faithfulness are perfected.*" Against all odds, God will see you through to the other side!

it dawned on me...

HeartLee, Cole, PresLee, Ashlon

"*Your sin will find you out.*" Numbers 32:23. This was one of my K5 memory verses and favorite lessons we learned over the years during my teaching career. So fitting this Fall season.

The story went something like this. One day a little boy and girl were told by their father to take a bag of pumpkin seeds down to the field to plant. But they wanted to go fishing instead and decided they would plant them later without him knowing. They stuck the bag of pumpkin seeds in an old rotten tree stump and ran off happily. After being tucked in the bed that night they remembered the seeds and decided to get up early and plant them. A storm came and it rained for several days and the children forgot about planting the pumpkin seeds. Weeks later when they remembered, they hoped their dad would not. The children were so nervous they began to have very scary nightmares about pumpkins coming into their bedroom. The pumpkins would say in an eerie voice, "Yooourr siiiin wiiillll fiiiind yoouu oouuttt!" The boy and his sister felt miserable, alone, and afraid. Months and months went by and the children could no longer hold their sin within. They confessed to their father about having never planted the seeds and how sorry they were.

But of course, the father already knew and forgave them. He noticed the seeds trying to sprout from the old stump and was just waiting for his children to tell him the truth.

We may sometime be able to hide the truth from the people around us, but nothing is ever hidden from God. In Hebrews 4:13 believers are given a wonderful promise, "*If we confess our sin, He is faithful and just to forgive us of our sin, and faithful to cleanse us from all unrighteousness.*" "*We cannot hide from God no matter how hard we try. For He knows all we think and do, we cannot escape His eye!*" Hebrews 4:13

it dawned on me...

"*For in Heaven, there is no mourning, crying pain or death. All things are made new.*" Revelation 21:4, 5 Many are missing someone special during the holiday season. They are longing to hold a loved one's hand, capture their smile again, or simply say, "I love you" one more time.

Find comfort in knowing that there is a real place that has been created by God for each of us. An extraordinary place of astounding wonder where pain and sorrow can never linger. Greater than we can fully imagine or understand is a place called Heaven.

My youngest daughter, PresLee writes - I was thinking about posting a cute Christmas picture on social media, but then my cousin sent this note to me. It was a note from my grandmother who passed away several years ago. To give you a little bit of a back story, someone had a seizure and drove their vehicle through my grandfather's house earlier this year. Today my uncle and cousin went to help clean up some of the debris and she found a note in a pile of broken chairs and tables. The letter was written by my grandmother, who we call Jam Jam.

My Mom

The fact that it is a letter about Christmas and Christmas is coming up in a few days just shows how God works in mysterious ways. Today,

God let our Grandmother speak to us and wish us Merry Christmas. My Christmas has already been made and most definitely the best one yet. This truly was a gift of love from God. I know my Jam Jam will be watching over our family this Christmas. She loves us, even if it is not heard, it is known. Forever continuing to love my Jam Jam. Philippians 4:13 – her favorite verse.

it dawned on me...

As a child, I remember watching "Mr. Rogers Neighborhood" and traveling on the trolley to the *The Land of Make Believe.* He was such an inspirational friend to many. Funny, I was always concerned about Mr. Rogers not being able to change his sweater and shoes in enough time before the song was over. He always seemed to tie that last shoe string in the nick of time. In one of the episodes he mentioned that sometimes it may seem like we are at the end of something, when in reality, we are at the beginning of something else. I find this intriguing.

I was once the Calendar Queen. Scheduling my family's life and recording activities both my daughters participated in, was crucial. I taped calendars on my cabinets in the kitchen and looked at them every morning. My life was a story about control, my control. Control of what I say and what I do. My control! Does that sound familiar?

God broke me of this quickly. Since, I have learned that someone else is calling the shots. Ultimately the one who controls all our ways and delays is the Lord. Even our time and schedules are in His hands. An unexpected or unwanted wait comes as no surprise to God. The Bible says in Proverbs 19:21, "*Many are the plans in a person's heart, but it is the Lord's purpose that prevails.*" Since my dad was in the military, we were transferred to numerous Air Force Bases year after year. I lived in about thirteen states and attended ten or more schools. Traveling was exciting, but I did not want instability for my daughters. My goal was to keep both at the same school until graduation. In this case it was the school that I taught at for nearly 30 years.

But that was not God's plan. Once again, we found ourselves packing for another move and another new school. "Why God? This is not on my Calendar! This is highly messing up my plans… again!"

If we could only trust God with the calendar of our lives. Isaiah 55:9 says, "*His ways are so much higher than our ways and His thoughts are so much higher than our thoughts.*" God sees the big picture from beginning to end. His plan is much better than ours and His outcome is for our good. Remember when Jesus pushed over the tables in the temple? Well, He tore down the calendars in my kitchen!

Sometimes He messes up our plans in order to get us to a new level. Sometimes that new level does not feel good at all. Sometimes God must tear down, so that He can rebuild. The good news is that God is a good Father. He wants what is best for us and has a perfect plan. In Isaiah 40:28 it says, "*He does not faint or grow weary; His understanding is unsearchable.*" How comforting it is to know that God sees all and has the perfect plan already mapped out for us. What makes us think we could do better? Many times, we are unaware as to the things God saves us from. So, it is important to trust the almighty, powerful God and stick to His calendar of life. He will not lead us to a land of make believe, for He has a greater purpose for all his children.

Ironically, I now get up every morning and take my orange T-Shirt off the hanger. I wear it as I teach online English classes to Chinese students. It's a beautiful day in this neighborhood.

it dawned on me...

God keeps His promises. It seems like yesterday when I taught my daughter, PresLee, in Kindergarten. The year was 2008. Back then, I knew she would graduate High School in the year of 2020. But that seemed so far away. Someone once told me not to blink because they grow up too fast.

And now it is 2020 - unbelievable how time flies. Little did I know she would not have a normal graduation due to some major changes that COVID- 19 brought about in our world. School closed in early March and she did not get to experience many things other seniors have treasured in the past such as, prom, Choir trip, Honors day, graduation, and more. There was quite a panic during the pandemic, people hoarding toilet paper and hand sanitizer, and more.

The pandemic caused quite an economic shock. A number of companies, workers, and families have been affected. Many people are nervous and afraid because the unknown is scary. Wearing masks have become fashion statements and are mandatory in many places and some restaurants are serving curb side. Obviously, everyone has spent a great deal of time trying to get used to the radical lifestyle change the virus brought. The pandemic resulted in what is effectively the largest work from home experiment ever conducted.

People are accessing more educational resources online for their kids; finding unconventional ways to connect with coworkers, friends, and family. And sadly, loved ones have contracted the virus and passed away.

Is it possible that our world has hit rock bottom? Are you afraid of the unknown? Are you in need of a miracle in these perilous times? It is important that we seek God daily with all our heart, with all our soul, and with all our mind. Remember that God loves you and is for you. You are His child. Just like your earthly father, when you fall and skin your knee, your heavenly Father picks you up and comforts you. God is bigger than the problems our world is facing. He is in the middle of this mess and is in control of all the chaos. Even if it does not look like it or feel like it, God is right beside you. He never grows tired or weary. He never sleeps. He is always working behind the scenes preparing a way. His timing is perfect.

Isaiah 43:18 says, "*Forget about all that, the past, everything that has happened. It is nothing compared to what I am going to do. For I am about to do something brand new in 2020. Don't you see, I've already begun. I will make a pathway through the wilderness; I will create rivers in the dry wastelands.*"

This is such a powerful word for all of us in this year of 2020. Instead of feeling as if this year has been a complete let down, we should allow the change in our world to grow us. Becoming more like Jesus Christ and how we respond and act in difficult situations, opens the door to His promises. Romans 8:28 says, "*And we know that all things work together for good to them that love God, to them who are the called according to His purpose.*" Sometimes difficult seasons linger and it's easy to feel discouraged. Just know, that God has not forgotten you. It's as if He is saying, "I have not forgotten about it my child. I will do it. I promise. It is coming. Look up, child. Trust me, love. Have peace, friend. You have nothing to fear, darling. I will not disappoint you, honey. I will not betray you. I will not forsake you. I will always love you. My promise still stands!"

Yes, sometimes we do have to hit rock bottom to find out who our rock really is…Jesus Christ!

it dawned on me...

That Gethsemane is a place of prayer. A couple of years ago I created a war room, so to speak, and my prayer life has completely changed. I taped Bible verses and different prayers all over the inside of my closet and spent many hours with God. I call it my war room because I spent a great amount of time wrestling with God.

Funny thing, my dogs were always in my closet with me, and many times a cat or two. I do believe they were all filled with the Holy Ghost and will one day make it to pet heaven. How could they not?

On a more serious note, try to picture Jesus falling to the ground in desperation in His Gethsemane before the soldiers took Him away. His soul was completely overwhelmed with sorrow to the point of death. He felt alone, afraid, and abandoned. Luke 22 says, He cried out in agony and sweated great drops of blood. He even cried out, "*If it is possible, take this cup from me. This is so hard; my flesh is weak.*" But Jesus knew that there was no other way to get Him to the place that He needed to be.

Have you ever found yourself in a place that felt so wrong: You may have felt alone, abandoned, and afraid? You may have cried out, "I don't want this to be a part of my story! Why did you allow this to happen to me God? Where are you? Have you forgotten me? Please take this away! Fix it! Why did you bring me here? Save me God!"

One thing I recently learned is this: even when things went wrong, it was right. In my mind right now, I can picture Jesus breaking the bread and dipping it, then passing it to Judas and saying, "Do what you must do." You know, sometimes God uses our loved ones, our friends, and even our enemies to go and do what they must do in order to get us where we need to be.

So, no matter where you are in life, no matter what battle you are facing, understand that Jesus has already been there. And just like Him, there is no other way to get you to the place that you need to be except for you to drink from this cup. I want to encourage you to get to your Gethsemane. Get to your war room and become a prayer warrior. We all have so many battles to fight. Do not go it alone. God will not leave your side and He will pick you up when you are too wounded to go on. Just as God raised His son from the grave. He will raise you up from the pit and put you in the palace. He is almighty and powerful. He has not forgotten you. It is amazing how impeccable God's timing is. So, do not give up in your Gethsemane today.

it dawned on me...

That He gives and He takes away. Once I heard a story about a little girl with an imitation pearl necklace. She thought it was the most beautiful thing she had ever seen. The girl wore the pearls everywhere she went. On her 16th birthday, her dad asked her to give him the pearls. But she just could not let the pearls go because she loved them so much. With tear-filled eyes, she finally handed them over to her father and he put the imitation pearls in his pocket. He then pulled out a blue velvet case with a strand of genuine pearls and handed them to his daughter.

He had been waiting for her to give up her counterfeit so that he could give her something even better, something authentic and real. I was this little girl. My grandmother once gave me some beautiful pearls when I was only 5 years of age. The pearls were longer than I was and had to be wrapped several times around my neck in order for me to wear them. I felt as beautiful as if I were a queen! I remember the day I wore the pearls to school. After playing on the playground, I realized the pearls had gotten tangled around my neck. I felt as if I were being choked.

My dad was called to the rescue and he worked diligently to untangle the pearls without having to cut the strand. It is amazing how something that I once treasured and thought so precious consumed me.

Today, I tearfully hand over my pearl necklace to my dear Father who has been patiently waiting on me. He wants to take away my counterfeit and give me something better, something genuine and real. Isaiah 43:19 says, "*See, I am doing a new thing! Now it springs up; do you not perceive it? I am making a way in the wilderness and streams in the wasteland.*" If God takes away something valuable to you that you never expected to lose, He will replace it doubly with something you never expected to have! And it will be so much better, an honest-to-goodness real thing!

it dawned on me...

Forgiveness is something we do for ourselves, not for others. In fact, when we forgive someone, we are really giving ourselves a gift. To forgive someone is to give up our right to vengeance.

It is interesting what David said about the sting of betrayal. It is found in Psalm 55:12, 13 "*If an enemy were insulting me, then I could endure it; If a foe were rising against me, then I could hide. But it is you, a man like myself, my companion, my close friend.*" David was no stranger to the torment of enemies, but even that seems less painful than betrayal from a friend.

I heard an amazing forgiveness story about Corrie Ten Boom. She and her family would hide Jews upstairs in their home in hopes to save them from concentration camps. When Nazi officers learned what was going on, they raided the house and Corrie was taken to a prison, a political concentration camp, and then a death camp. Miraculously, she survived.

As you can imagine there were many hardships that she had to overcome even after the war. One such moment was many years later, at a church. She saw a man from a distance who began making his way towards her. He reached out his hand as if he wanted to shake her hand. Corrie recognized him as one of the guards in the concentration camp where her sister had died. Immediately the painful memories overwhelmed her. She knew that she could not reach out her hand in her own strength. He did not recognize Corrie, but she knew exactly who he was.

Corrie often spoke of the need to forgive others. But this time she wrestled with the most difficult thing she ever had to do. We must understand that the message that God forgives has a prior condition: that we forgive those who have injured us. "If you do not forgive men their trespasses," Jesus says, "neither will your Father in heaven forgive your trespasses." (Matthew 6:14-15)

This is a hard pill to swallow. Those who can forgive are able to move forward and rebuild their lives. But those who nurse their bitterness remain stuck and unable to obtain joy. God gave Corrie the strength to not only forgive the man but also to love him. She slowly reached out her hand and at that moment she could feel the love and forgiveness flow from her hand to his.

Is there someone you need to forgive today? Then take courage from Corrie Ten Boom. She once said, "Forgiveness is the key to unlock the door of resentment and the handcuffs of hatred. It is a power that breaks the chains of bitterness and the shackles of selfishness." Jesus taught that loving our neighbor as ourselves is important. "*But I tell you, love your enemies, bless them that curse you, do good to them that hate you, and pray for them which despitefully use you.*" Matthew 5:4 It is extremely difficult to forgive someone who has betrayed you. Luke 18:27 says, "*It is only possible with God.*"

God's love for us is unconditional and undeserving and only with His love can we love and pray for those who hurt us. Do not waste minutes on what does not matter. Life is too short.

it dawned on me...

That Habakkuk stands for "wrestle and embrace". I remember not too long ago when both of my daughters saw the rug being pulled out from under me and I was just lying there on the ground. I told them, "This is what rock bottom looks like."

Rock bottom is where you find God, even if you already know Him. And even if you already have a relationship with Him, this is the place where you seek Him with all your heart. No, ifs, ands, or buts about it. It is the lowest level that you do not want anyone to see, but it is impossible to hide. It's when you are right smack at Jesus' feet, completely broken and holding on for dear life. Its wanting to die but continuing to live. There is no appetite and you are eating only to survive. It's begging God for answers and angry at Him for allowing it to happen. It is not casual, quiet conversation with God, but it is crucial, critical, crying out loud to the only One who can take you in the palm of His hands and put you back together again.

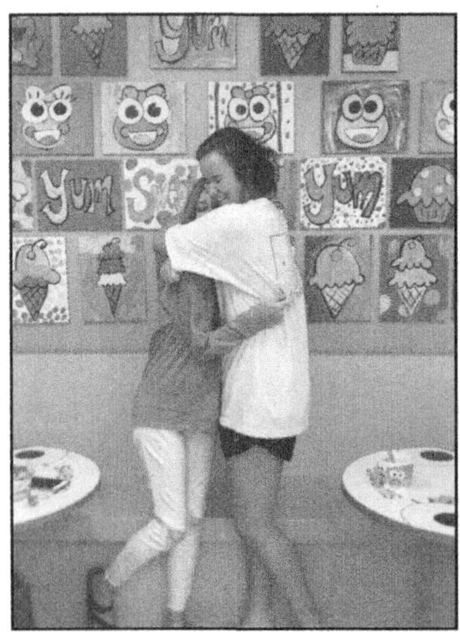

Me and Pres

Habakkuk 1:2 says, *"How long, Lord, must I call for help, but you do not listen?"* This sounds like me wrestling with God in my war room. So, I officially changed my name to Habakkuk today. Seriously, I did develop a close relationship with Habakkuk during some of my most difficult times. I read this verse repeatedly for many months: Habakkuk 3:17-18 "*Though the fig tree does not bud and there are no grapes on the vines, though the olive crop fails and the fields produce no food, though there are no sheep in the pen and no cattle in the stalls, yet I will rejoice in the Lord, I will be joyful in God my Savior.*"

I know God hears me, but the process is just so long. It feels like an eternity. I made my war room and pretty much lived in it. I would teach online classes very early each morning, hiding behind a smile. With the last goodbye I'd run as fast as I could to my war room and fall to my knees crying out to God. Wrestling with God and carrying a ton of emotions. Humiliation, brokenness, unworthiness, embarrassment, were emotions that tormented my soul.

But this is where my testimony begins. If I had never felt my life was over then I would never have learned how to pray, really pray. If I had never been abandoned, then I would have never learned to depend utterly upon my Lord. If I had never been betrayed, then I would have never run so hard into the arms of Jesus. He is truly my Jehovah Jireh, my provider.

I thank Him for my journey because if what happened, never happened, I do not know what my relationship with God would be like today. Psalm 46:1-3 says, "*God is our refuge and strength, an ever-present help in trouble. Therefore, we will not fear, though the earth gives way and the mountains fall into the heart of the sea, though its waters roar and foam and the mountains quake with their surging. There is a river whose streams make glad the city of God, the holy place where the Most High dwells. God is within her; she will not fall; God will help her at the break of day.*" Isaiah 41:10 says, "*So do not fear, for I am with you; do not be dismayed, for I am your God. I will strengthen you and help you; I will uphold you with my righteous right hand.*"

There is a God in heaven, one who cares and one who sees all. You can find strength, renewal, and rely on God's power when life does not always go as planned. Yes, God could have healed me in one second, but the process was too important to skip. In order to get me where I needed to be, in order to grow me, I had to learn to embrace my life and praise Him no matter what. Wrestle, embrace, wrestle, embrace, wrestle, embrace! God really does have our best interest at heart. And God's timing is never late. He is always on time.

it dawned on me...

photo by Katie Byrd

That sometimes being uncomfortable is for our own good. It is interesting that an eagle builds its nest high in the tallest trees and the highest mountain edges. Many who have observed this majestic bird constructing its home say that it first lays down briars, jagged stone, and all kinds of sharp objects, which would seem unsuited for its purpose. And then the eagle covers the structure with a thick layer of wool, feathers and fur of animals.

This makes a nesting place soft and comfortable, a delightful sanctuary where the eagle may hatch its young. In Deuteronomy 32:11, 12 it says, "*Like an eagle that stirs up its nest and hovers over its young, that spreads its wings to catch them and carries them aloft.*" The eaglets will not remain in the inviting cradle for long. The day will come when the mother will stir up the nest just like in Deuteronomy and those prickly things will start making them feel very uncomfortable. The eagle will begin to tear away some of the soft cushioning they have had for a long time. The eaglets will begin to feel pain and struggle to get out on their own and fly. This is the mother's objective. She is not being cruel but instinctively producing discontent with the old life of ease and spurring them on to full development.

Wow! This is amazing. It is a picture of how the Lord promotes growth in us. He often sends or uses adversity and trying times just to rouse us from our complacency so that we can move on to maturity in Christ. It is interesting that strength comes from struggle and weakness from ease. If the sharp thorns and stones of affliction are irritating you, it is God's grace designed to activate you. A stirred-up nest is a token of His special love. God loves us so much and wants the best for us. His ways are higher than our ways. His thoughts are higher than ours. He has so many great things planned for us but at times must remove us from our comfort zone to get our attention. Sometimes we must feel those sharp pains, those uncomfortable and hurting moments to get us to the place we need to be.

I want to encourage you today to spread your wings of faith and soar to new heights of blessings.

it dawned on me...

That God must be trying to teach me lessons through birds. I have had many bird incidents happen in my lifetime and the birds were not always little and cute. Many times, they were extremely large and deep down I was petrified.

artwork by PresLee

One morning around 6:00, while in the kitchen, I heard a very strange and loud commotion in the backyard. I ran outside and looked up into the sky. It was a murmuration, what seemed to be millions of birds flying very close together. The sound that they made was spectacular. It was truly mesmerizing. The birds were flying in swooping, intricately coordinated patterns through the sky. It was incredibly cool.

I felt like God wanted me to take in the beauty of this moment, so I just watched and listened. The birds seemed so focused on where they were going, and nothing seemed to get in their way. It was as if they were 'one' and God was directing them. The birds flew with expectation. Since then, I have learned that a murmuration is like a bird dance, an aerial ballet with tens and thousands of starlings, grackles, cowbirds, and redwing blackbirds flying in mass, but seemingly in one mind.

I now understand that birds do this because grouping together offers safety in numbers and they gather to keep warm at night. This reminds me of Matthew 6:26, "*Look at the birds of the air, they neither sow nor reap, nor gather into barns; yet your Heavenly Father feeds them. Are you not of more value than they?*" I am thankful that I had the chance to encounter one of nature's greatest and most fleeting phenomena.

Every year I told my kindergarten students the story of the 10 lepers and the healing of the bird on our playground. The very next year my students insisted that I tell the story over and over and over. I must have told that story one hundred times because it was their favorite.

I will never forget, on the last day of school, my students and their parents and I planned a big graduation celebration at the park. Everyone was carrying bags of food and rolling ice chests to the pavilion to prepare for lunch. Frantically, some of the students ran over to me and grabbed my arm. They said that there was a hurt bird in the trashcan. Of course, when I get there, I notice it is not a teeny, tiny bird but a huge black buzzard looking thing. Its wing was completely matted in some type of glue trap. The bird was weak from trying to get unstuck, and the wing was a mangled mess. The kids said, "lets pray for it like your K-5 class did last year". In my mind I thought, "Oh no, here we go again." And this time there were parents to witness the event.

By the grace of God, I managed to get the poor Pterodactyl out of the trashcan and on to the ground, where we proceeded to pick its wing out of the glue. With every careful pull and pry, the wing would break. It seemed that I was doing more damage than good. Finally, we were able to free the bird from the glue trap. Its wing was so broken and in the natural eye to us adults, seemed like a hopeless case.

Nevertheless, we all gathered around the bird in a big circle, parents included and prayed. I should have had all the faith in the world due to the last bird healing. I knew God could, but just not sure He would, a second time around. Furthermore, I felt extremely unqualified to pray around parents. But the kids were already prepared for a miracle. As I prayed, a small breeze lifted the wings a bit. I began to pray in my mind for God to send a big breeze that would pick the bird up from the ground. My students started softly chanting, "I believe Jesus can, I believe Jesus can, I believe Jesus can." Another small breeze lifted the wings a bit more and the students chanted louder, "I believe Jesus can, I believe Jesus can, I believe Jesus can." Suddenly the bird tried to fly, and everyone began to shout, "I believe Jesus can, I believe Jesus can, I believe Jesus can.

Believe it or not a huge gust of wind came through, picking up the bird in the air and it began to fly! My students and I were cheering, parents were crying, for we had just experienced an amazing miracle from the Lord. Of course, we all gathered back around in a circle and thanked God for answering our prayer. While the kids played T- ball on the field that afternoon, we noticed the big bird flying in circles over us as if to say, "Thank you." Look what our God can do! And yes, a second time too!

it dawned on me...

That God keeps His promises. One of my favorite Bible stories as a child was Noah's Ark. I think about the great faith Noah must have had to build the ark when it had never even rained before. Many mocked and laughed at him, that is, until the first drop of rain fell. Drip, drop, drip, drop. Oh, no!

God knew the sinful state of the world was self-destructive and loved the world enough to intervene. His plan ultimately provided a way for you and me to come to salvation. God sees the bigger picture, so we must trust Him even when we do not understand His ways. My favorite part of the story is when God placed a colorful rainbow in the sky for all to see. Genesis 9:11 says, "*This is my promise to you: All life on the earth was destroyed by the flood. But that will never happen again.*"

You know, God desires to have a relationship with His children. He longs for you to take time out of your busy day and spend time with Him. Do not let the cares of the world interfere with the One who holds the world in His hands.

It is never too late for new beginnings. I have learned the importance of talking with God and I honestly could not do life without Him. I am not my own and I will not live as such. But there was a time when I was weary, and all prayed out. I did not know what to say anymore and I felt like a broken record. So, one day at work I Googled different prayers and got a few from some books that I had read. I made copies and covered them with contact paper and left them on my desk in a pile while I went to lunch.

When I returned, my co-worker and good friend, Kitoria asked if I would make her some prayers too. Of course, I did, but didn't want to hand her a pile of prayers that could be dropped and scattered about. So, I punched a hole in the corner and made a decorative cover. I had some big hooped earrings I'd never worn and attached the prayers to the ring. She loved it! In fact, another co-worker approached me wanting what she called a "Ring of Prayers".

Needless to say, I spent many hours making these newly named "Ring of Prayer" books. The books were made to add new prayers at any time and a place to write down prayer requests for others. I eventually made myself a "Ring of Prayers", a "Ring of Praise", a "Ring of Declarations", and a "Ring of Living Verses". Yes, my prayer life has definitely grown and changed for the better. 1 Thessalonians 5:16 says, "*Rejoice always, pray without ceasing, give thanks in all circumstances, for this is the will of God in Christ Jesus for you.*"

Did you know that you can bring anything to God, no matter how big or small? I remember writing down some needs in my prayer book and praying continually. College tuitions for both my daughters were due and my youngest needed a laptop and the list went on and on. I have learned to lay my cares and concerns at God's feet believing that He will meet my every need. Nothing is too big or small for Him. He is always working, and we do not have to figure it all out. Just spend time with Jesus and expect Him to show up. Psalm 5:3 says, "*In the morning, oh Lord, you hear my voice; I lay my requests before you and wait in expectation.*"

How wonderful! I will never forget the day my oldest daughter contacted me and said her tuition would be completely paid for and in the same moment, I received a text that a laptop would soon be sent to my youngest daughter. How amazing! Praise God! I knew God could do it but was not sure how He would do it. A few minutes later my daughter PresLee messaged me and said we had a bag of vegetables hanging on our front doorknob. Who knew God made home deliveries too! It was actually my sweet neighbors, Sue and Jerry, who brought me some home-grown veggies. God is so good. On my way home from work I was filled with joy and thankfulness. When I turned in to my driveway, I saw the most beautiful rainbow in the sky. God always keeps His promises!

it dawned on me...

That there is a little bit of Paris in Prattville. Padlocks have become decorative art along the railing of the popular Creek Walk downtown. The public walkway follows the creek that Daniel Pratt first used to power his mill where he manufactured cotton gins. Though the mills are abandoned, the building and spillways still exist, making a picturesque site for couples and families.

Some locks are plain, but most contain initials, a date stamp or a personalized message. In the 2013 film, *Now You See Me*, the final scene shows a bridge railing in Paris covered in padlocks. The Pont des Arts pedestrian bridge is real, as was its Locks of Love custom.

One of my close friends, Amanda and I have both gone through similar life situations that we never anticipated. Not too long ago she and her daughters visited, and we enjoyed making some more special memories as we walked downtown.

Both my daughters and hers placed a lock on the railing today as if to say, "Today, I close the door to my past, open the door to my future, take a deep breath and start a new chapter in my life." After putting the lock on the railing, the key was thrown into the water below. "*Forgetting what lies behind and straining forward to what lies ahead.*" Philippians 3:13

As I look back on my life, I realize that every time I thought I was being rejected from something good, I was being redirected to something better. Remember, God has your best interest at heart. When a door closes you do not know what God is saving you from. Rejection is… God's protection.

So, for now, I am saying goodbye to my past and welcoming a New Year!

it dawned on me...

That cousin fun is the best kind of fun ever. I know my daughters have an unbreakable bond with all their cousins. Oh, the memories of going to the beach, making up dance videos and tutorials on YouTube, and staying up all night. There is nothing better than cousin love. I can testify to this and will never forget the many times my grandmother would put a big mattress in the middle of the floor, and my cousins and I would do flips and back handsprings on it. And oh, what fun we had playing the card games Old Maid and Go Fish! We also enjoyed taking walks around the neighborhood and visiting spooky, old graveyards.

Speaking of graveyards, if you have ever noticed on a headstone, in most cases there is the deceased's name, date of birth, and date of death inscribed on them, along with a personal message, or prayers. The dash that is on the gravestone represents the time on earth between the date of birth and the date of death.

That little line on the headstone is significant because the dash represents all the time they spent alive on earth and now only those who loved them know what that little line is worth. James 4:14 says, "*What is your life? For you are a mist that appears for a little time and then vanishes.*" Psalm 103:15 says, "*As for man, his days are like grass; he flourishes like a flower of the field; for the wind passes over it, and it is gone, and its place knows it no more.*" Life is what happens in the dash between the dates.

How do you want to be remembered? What will your legacy be? In 2 Timothy 4, the apostle Paul stated his legacy. His turbulent life

was coming to an end, but he had truly made a difference. Paul said, "*I have fought the good fight. I have finished the race; I have kept the faith. Finally, there is laid up for me the crown of righteousness, which the Lord, the righteous Judge, will give to me on that day, and not to me only but also to all who have loved His appearing.*"

Our goal should be to make it across the finish line and have an abundant entrance into the kingdom of God. You are running a race. Keep running. If you slowed down, it is time to move forward because you will leave a legacy. What will you be known for? What will your children, family and friends remember you for? Your life can truly make a difference if you are on the right course.

God calls every one of us to finish every task with excellence because if you think about it, every task and every day could be your last. The best way that we can finish the race is to live faithfully in union with Jesus Christ, so that, someday, when we enter God's kingdom, we will receive the crown of righteousness that Jesus Christ gives to us when He will say those seven words, "Well done, my good and faithful servant."

When you take your final breath, what will your dash say about your life?

it dawned on me...

That God gets the glory out of my story! When I wrote this book, I did not know if anyone would want to read it. I prayed continually if only one person came to know Jesus Christ as their personal Savior, it would be worth it all.

One of the most important things I have learned and hope to leave with you is to walk by faith and not by sight. Remember, you can never please God without faith, without depending on Him. Anyone who wants to come to God must believe that there is a God and that He rewards those who sincerely look for Him. (Hebrews 11:6)

David, Daun, Dad

In the Bible, Job is presented as a good and prosperous family man who is beset by Satan, with God's permission, with horrendous disasters that take away all that he holds dear, including his offspring, his health, and his property. He struggles to understand his situation and begins a search for the answers to his difficulties. In Job 23:8-9 Job cries out, "*Behold I go forward, but He is not there, and backward, but I do not perceive Him; on the left hand when He is working, I do not behold Him; he turns to the right hand, but I do not see Him.*"

You may be able to relate to the emotional, physical and spiritual struggle that Job is wrestling with in these verses. In other words, he is saying, "God I'm walking forward, but I don't see you, you're not there. I'm looking backwards God, but I don't perceive you and I don't understand what you're doing. When I look forward, I don't understand it either. I look to the left and have faith to believe that You are working and doing something, but I just can't see it. I turn to the right, God, but You are not there."

In all of Job's distress he did not stop there. If nothing else, grab this verse. He makes this declaration, "*But, He knows the way that I take; when He has tried me, I shall come out as gold!*" Job 23:10

Wow! Such amazing faith! You may be facing a pandemic, financial strain, sickness, abandonment, or maybe all hell has broken loose. You may say, "God I'm running to You, but I don't see You. I look back but I do not perceive You. When I look to the left and the right, I can't find you, God." Does this describe your situation? You may be tired and weary. Everything around you looks hopeless and dead, or like me, the weight/wait of hope is even too heavy to bear. It is in this moment you can set your faith on the promise and declare – "But He knows the way that I take; when He has tried me, I shall come out as gold." In other words, I am going to keep going and when I do, I will come out as gold!

In order to have faith, one must move. Faith without works is dead. Just ask God for wisdom, knowledge, and understanding. Invest your time and energy in God and His purpose for your life. God is waiting on us to move, so do your part and God will meet you halfway. During life's most difficult situations, God will bring a level of joy, peace, and strength out of the middle of it all. When the test is over, when the trying is over, this one declaration I'm going to declare, "But He knows the way that I take; when He has tried me, I shall come out as gold!"

Made in the USA
Monee, IL
08 November 2020

47006490R00108